AF446913

The Edge Where Desire Breaks

What Happens When the Heart Takes Over

Zachary Ball

The Edge Where Desire Breaks 1

What Happens When the Heart Takes Over 1

Zachary Ball 1

Chapter 1: The Anatomy of Desire 5

    The Science of Longing: How Desire Shapes Us 5

    Emotional Triggers What Ignites the Fire 8

    Vulnerability and Attraction: The Hidden Connection 13

    The Role of Fantas When the Mind Takes Control 17

    When Cravings Collide with Reality 22

Chapter 2: The Power Struggle Between Heart and Mind 27

    Logic vs Emotion The Eternal Tug of War 27

    The Rational Minds Retreat When Emotions Win 31

    The Impulsive Heart Acting Without Thinking 36

    The Role of Past Experiences in Emotional Decisions 41

    Breaking Free from Emotional Sabotage 46

Chapter 3: The Breaking Point of Desire 52

    Recognizing the Edge When Desire Becomes All Consuming 52

    Obsession vs Passion Knowing the Difference 57

    The Cost of Losing Control: When Desire Takes Over 62

    Red Flags in the Pursuit of Longing 66

    The Emotional Fallout of Unchecked Desire 71

Chapter 4: Love and Lust Where They Collide 77

    The Thin Line Between Lust and Love 77

    Chemistry and Compatibility Do They Go Hand in Hand 81

    Physical Needs vs Emotional Fulfillment 86

    The Role of Time When Lust Evolves into Love 91

    The Hearts Decision Choosing Love Over Desire 95

Chapter 5: Desire in Modern Relationships 101

    Technology and Temptation The Role of Digital Love 101

Open Relationships Redefining Desire in the 21st Century .106

Social Medias Influence on Emotional Cravings.................... 110

The Struggle for Authentic Connection in a Superficial World
.... 115

The Future of Love and Desire in an Ever Changing Landscape
.... 121

Chapter 1: The Anatomy of Desire

The Science of Longing: How Desire Shapes Us

Desire is an intrinsic part of the human condition, a potent force that has shaped civilizations, driven personal ambition, and even altered the course of history. It is neither inherently good nor bad, but its influence is undeniable. From the yearning for personal connection to the pursuit of material wealth or intellectual fulfillment, desire propels us forward, often dictating the trajectory of our lives. To truly understand the power of longing and how it shapes us, we must delve into its roots—where biology, psychology, and societal constructs converge.

At its core, desire stems from the brain's reward system, a complex network designed to keep us motivated and ensure survival. The neurotransmitter dopamine plays a pivotal role in this process. Contrary to popular belief, dopamine is not the chemical of pleasure but of anticipation. It surges when we anticipate something rewarding, whether it's a warm embrace, a well-cooked meal, or the thrill of a professional achievement. This anticipation pushes us to act, to move toward the object of our yearning. Without this mechanism, humans might lack the drive to pursue even basic needs, let alone more abstract goals.

Desire, however, is not limited to physical survival. While hunger, thirst, and shelter are primal needs, the human experience expands far beyond these basics. We crave connection, validation, and meaning. Psychologically, these longings are closely tied to Maslow's hierarchy of needs, a framework that categorizes human motivations. Beyond the physiological and safety levels lie love and belonging, esteem, and self-actualization. Desire is the thread that connects these levels, weaving its way through our relationships, our aspirations, and our identities.

Social and cultural influences also shape our desires. From an early age, we are conditioned by our environments—family, media, peers, and societal norms. These external factors subtly dictate what we yearn for and how we define fulfillment. In some cultures, desire may manifest as the pursuit of individual success, while in others, it may lean toward collective harmony or spiritual enlightenment. These cultural constructs do not merely reflect our desires; they actively mold and reshape them, often creating a feedback loop where longing is reinforced by societal validation.

Our emotional triggers further complicate the landscape of desire. Past experiences, whether positive or negative, shape our emotional responses and influence our future cravings. For instance, a person who felt neglected as a child may develop a heightened longing for affection and validation in adulthood. Similarly, someone who experienced financial hardship might channel their desire into accumulating wealth as a means of security. These emotional imprints can be both empowering and limiting, providing a framework for growth or a trap of recurring, unfulfilled yearnings.

The role of fantasy cannot be overlooked when examining how desire shapes us. The human mind has a remarkable capacity for imagination, allowing us to envision futures that may never come to pass. Fantasizing about what could be—whether it's a dream job, a romantic partner, or a life of adventure—fuels our motivation. Yet, this same capacity can create a tension between reality and expectation. The gap between what we have and what we long for can lead to dissatisfaction, frustration, and even despair. Striking a balance between ambition and contentment is a delicate act, one that requires self-awareness and emotional maturity.

Interestingly, desire is not static; it evolves over time. What we crave in our youth often differs from what we seek in middle age or later life. This shift is influenced by life experiences, changing priorities, and a deeper understanding of ourselves. For example, the impulsive desires of adolescence, driven by hormonal changes and a quest for identity, may give way to more measured aspirations as we age. In this sense, desire serves as both a mirror and a map, reflecting who we are at a given moment while guiding us toward who we wish to become.

While desire is often viewed as a personal experience, it also has a profound social dimension. Group dynamics, for instance, can amplify individual longing. The phenomenon of "social proof" demonstrates how people are more likely to desire something if they see others valuing it. This can be seen in trends, whether it's a new technology, a fashion statement, or even a social cause. The collective validation of a desire can make it feel more urgent and compelling, sometimes at the expense of personal authenticity.

Despite its many facets, desire is not without its pitfalls. When unchecked, it can become all-consuming, leading to obsession and a loss of perspective. The pursuit of unbridled longing can strain relationships, compromise ethics, and even harm mental health. This is particularly true in cases where desire is rooted in external validation rather than intrinsic fulfillment. A person who seeks approval from others may find themselves trapped in a cycle of perpetual striving, never quite satisfied regardless of their achievements.

On the flip side, desire also has the power to transform. It is a catalyst for growth, innovation, and self-discovery. Many of humanity's greatest accomplishments—from artistic masterpieces to scientific breakthroughs—were fueled by a deep and unwavering longing. Desire challenges us to step out of our comfort zones, to take risks, and to confront our fears. In this way, it serves as a double-edged sword, capable of both destruction and creation.

Emotional Triggers What Ignites the Fire

Human emotions are intricate, layered, and often unpredictable, but they are the foundation of what makes us who we are. At the very core of these emotions are triggers—specific stimuli that ignite reactions and create ripples in our inner world. Emotional triggers can be subtle or overwhelming, fleeting or long-lasting, but their influence is undeniable when it comes to shaping the desires that drive our decisions and actions. Understanding what ignites this fire is essential for recognizing the forces that guide our lives, often without our conscious awareness.

Emotional triggers are deeply tied to our personal history, experiences, and perceptions of the world. They are not random; they are imprints left by moments that have either enriched or wounded us. For instance, a song playing on the radio might evoke a flood of longing because it was the soundtrack to a cherished memory. Alternatively, a sharp tone of voice might trigger defensiveness if it reminds someone of past criticism. These triggers are deeply personal, yet their power lies in how they connect the past to the present, often magnifying our desires or fears in ways we don't immediately understand.

One of the most potent forms of emotional triggering comes from relationships. Human beings are inherently social creatures, and our interactions with others have a profound impact on our emotional landscape. A compliment from a stranger might light up feelings of self-worth, while a dismissive gesture from a loved one can plunge someone into self-doubt. These reactions are not simply about the present moment but are often tied to a person's deeper need for connection, acceptance, and validation. Emotional triggers in relationships have the ability to amplify desires—whether it's the longing for love, the need to be understood, or the yearning for harmony.

Another key element of emotional triggers lies in the sights, sounds, and smells of our environment. Sensory experiences are powerful catalysts for emotion because they bypass rational thought and speak directly to the subconscious mind. The scent of a familiar perfume can instantly transport someone to a passionate romance from years ago, while the sight of a particular location might stir a sense of yearning for adventure or escape. These sensory triggers often ignite desires that feel visceral and immediate, even if they stem from a long-buried memory or unfulfilled aspiration.

Cultural and societal influences also play a significant role in shaping emotional triggers. From a young age, individuals are exposed to societal norms and ideals that often dictate what they should value and desire. Advertisements, for instance, are masters at exploiting triggers to create longing for a product or lifestyle. A commercial showing a group of friends laughing together over drinks might tap into someone's emotional need for belonging, making them associate happiness with the specific brand being marketed. Social media has amplified this effect exponentially, with curated images and posts designed to evoke envy, admiration, or aspiration. These external triggers fuel desires that may not even originate from within but feel intensely personal.

Trauma and past experiences are perhaps the most deeply ingrained sources of emotional triggers. When someone has been hurt or betrayed, their brain becomes wired to recognize and react to similar situations in the future. This reaction is not just psychological but physiological, as the brain's amygdala—the center for processing emotions like fear and anger—goes into overdrive. For instance, a person who has experienced abandonment may develop a heightened sensitivity to rejection, causing them to react strongly to even minor signs of disinterest. These triggers not only shape how individuals respond to the world but also influence the desires they prioritize, such as a longing for security or the avoidance of vulnerability.

Beyond the personal realm, collective experiences can serve as powerful emotional triggers. Shared events, whether joyous or tragic, have the ability to unite people through common feelings and longings. For example, a community rallying together after a natural disaster might ignite a collective desire for resilience and support. Similarly, national celebrations or global movements can trigger feelings of pride, hope, or determination. These collective emotions create a shared sense of purpose and often amplify individual desires by connecting them to something larger than oneself.

The role of emotional triggers in desire is not limited to external stimuli; internal factors play an equally crucial part. Thoughts, beliefs, and expectations can serve as triggers that either ignite or suppress longing. For instance, someone who believes they are unworthy of love might react defensively to a romantic gesture, pushing away the very connection they secretly crave. In contrast, a person with a strong sense of self-worth might interpret the same gesture as validation of their desirability. These internal triggers are shaped by self-perception and can either empower or derail the pursuit of what one desires most.

Recognizing emotional triggers is the first step toward understanding their impact on desire. Self-awareness allows individuals to identify the stimuli that provoke strong emotional reactions and examine the underlying reasons for their intensity. For example, someone who notices they feel an inexplicable rush of envy when seeing a friend's vacation photos might uncover a suppressed longing for freedom or adventure. By acknowledging this desire, they can take actionable steps to incorporate more exploration into their own life, rather than simply reacting to the trigger with frustration or self-pity.

Managing emotional triggers requires a combination of mindfulness, emotional regulation, and intentional action. Mindfulness involves observing one's emotional reactions without judgment, creating space to respond thoughtfully rather than impulsively. Emotional regulation techniques, such as deep breathing or journaling, can help individuals process their feelings and gain clarity about what they truly desire. Finally, intentional action involves channeling the energy of emotional triggers into constructive pursuits. For instance, someone who feels a surge of longing when seeing a couple holding hands might use that feeling as motivation to strengthen their own relationships or seek new connections.

While emotional triggers can sometimes feel overwhelming, they also hold immense potential for growth and self-discovery. They act as mirrors, reflecting back the aspects of life that matter most to us. By paying attention to what ignites the fire within, individuals can gain a deeper understanding of their values, priorities, and aspirations. Emotional triggers are not obstacles to be avoided but opportunities to explore the depths of desire and uncover the truths that lie beneath the surface.

Vulnerability and Attraction: The Hidden Connection

Vulnerability is often misunderstood. It's frequently perceived as a weakness, an exposure to potential harm, something to be avoided or hidden. Yet, in the intricate dance of human connection, vulnerability is one of the most potent forces driving attraction. It's the silent thread that weaves intimacy into relationships, allowing two people to move beyond superficiality and into something genuine and profound. The link between vulnerability and attraction is not only powerful but also deeply rooted in our psychological and emotional makeup, shaping how we relate to one another and how we navigate love and desire.

Attraction is often portrayed as a surface-level phenomenon, sparked by physical appearances or shared interests. While these factors certainly play a role, they are only part of the story. True attraction—the kind that lingers, deepens, and withstands the test of time—requires something more. It requires a sense of authenticity and connection, which can only be achieved when both individuals allow themselves to be seen for who they truly are. This is where vulnerability enters the picture. To be vulnerable is to strip away the masks and defenses we use to shield ourselves from judgment or rejection, revealing our fears, hopes, and imperfections. It is in this raw, unguarded state that we become most relatable and, paradoxically, most magnetic.

The reason vulnerability is so integral to attraction can be traced back to the human need for connection. People are drawn to others who make them feel understood and accepted. When someone exposes their vulnerabilities, they create a space for empathy and compassion. For instance, imagine a confident, seemingly perfect individual who suddenly opens up about a personal struggle or a past failure. That moment of honesty can make them feel more approachable, more human, and, ultimately, more attractive. It's not their perfection that draws others in; it's their willingness to share their imperfections.

This connection between vulnerability and attraction is not just anecdotal but supported by psychological research. Studies on human relationships consistently show that self-disclosure—sharing personal thoughts, feelings, and experiences—fosters intimacy and strengthens bonds. When we share something meaningful about ourselves, it invites the other person to do the same, creating a cycle of mutual trust and understanding. This dynamic is particularly evident in romantic relationships, where vulnerability acts as a bridge to deeper emotional intimacy. Without it, relationships often remain shallow, driven by external factors rather than genuine connection.

However, the act of being vulnerable is not without its challenges. It requires courage, as it involves taking a risk—a risk of rejection, judgment, or misunderstanding. This is why many people hesitate to be vulnerable, especially in the context of attraction. They fear that exposing their true selves might push others away. Yet, the opposite is often true. While a façade of invulnerability might initially seem appealing, it can create a barrier that prevents genuine connection. People are not drawn to perfection; they are drawn to authenticity. The willingness to be vulnerable signals confidence—not the confidence of being flawless, but the confidence of being comfortable with one's own imperfections.

The interplay between vulnerability and attraction is particularly evident in the early stages of a relationship. When two people meet, there is often a natural inclination to present the best version of themselves. They focus on their strengths, downplay their weaknesses, and tread carefully to avoid saying or doing anything that might make them seem less appealing. While this is a natural part of human interaction, it can also create a sense of disconnection. If both individuals are too guarded, the relationship may struggle to move beyond surface-level attraction. On the other hand, when one person takes the leap to be vulnerable, it can pave the way for a deeper connection. A simple admission of nervousness, a candid story about a past mistake, or a heartfelt expression of feelings can transform the dynamic, making it more genuine and meaningful.

Interestingly, vulnerability does not only create attraction in romantic contexts but also in friendships, family relationships, and even professional settings. In all these areas, the willingness to be open and authentic fosters trust and connection. In fact, leaders who show vulnerability often inspire greater loyalty and respect from their teams, as it humanizes them and makes them more relatable. Similarly, friends who share their struggles and fears tend to form stronger, more enduring bonds than those who keep their interactions light and superficial.

Despite its power, vulnerability is not about oversharing or exposing oneself indiscriminately. There is a fine line between healthy vulnerability and emotional unburdening. True vulnerability involves sharing in a way that is thoughtful, intentional, and appropriate to the context. For example, revealing personal insecurities during a first date might create a sense of connection, but overwhelming the other person with deeply personal or unresolved issues could have the opposite effect. The key lies in finding a balance—being open enough to foster intimacy without crossing into territory that feels overwhelming or inappropriate.

Another important aspect of vulnerability is recognizing and respecting the vulnerability of others. Attraction is not a one-sided phenomenon; it is a mutual experience. Just as we long for others to see and accept our true selves, they long for the same from us. When someone shares their vulnerabilities, it is a gift—a sign that they trust us enough to let down their guard. Responding with empathy, kindness, and understanding not only strengthens the connection but also reinforces the cycle of mutual vulnerability and attraction.

Cultural and societal norms can also influence how vulnerability is perceived and expressed. In some cultures, showing vulnerability is seen as a strength, a sign of emotional intelligence and self-awareness. In others, it may be viewed as a weakness, something to be hidden or suppressed. These cultural attitudes can shape how individuals approach vulnerability in their relationships and, by extension, how they experience attraction. For instance, someone raised in an environment that values stoicism and emotional restraint may struggle to open up, even if they deeply desire connection. Overcoming these barriers often requires self-reflection, emotional growth, and, sometimes, the guidance of trusted friends, mentors, or therapists.

The Role of Fantas When the Mind Takes Control

Fantasies are the unspoken landscapes of the human mind, where desires, fears, and possibilities converge in infinite variations. They are not bound by the constraints of reality, allowing the mind to explore what could be, rather than what simply is. Whether fleeting or recurring, these mental images and scenarios play a pivotal role in shaping our emotions, decisions, and relationships. When the mind takes control through fantasy, it creates a realm where boundaries dissolve, and longing takes on a life of its own. At its core, fantasy is a reflection of our deepest desires, an unfiltered glimpse of what we yearn for, even when we cannot—or dare not—pursue it in the tangible world.

The power of fantasy lies in its ability to provide an escape. Life is often riddled with limitations: societal expectations, personal fears, and external circumstances that seem immovable. Fantasy, however, knows no such barriers. It offers a safe space to imagine outcomes that feel unattainable or even forbidden. A person stuck in a monotonous routine might daydream about a life of adventure and freedom, while someone yearning for connection might fantasize about a perfect relationship where every need is met without conflict. These imagined scenarios serve as a coping mechanism, alleviating the weight of unmet desires while temporarily satisfying the longing for something more.

However, the role of fantasy extends beyond mere escapism. It is also a tool for exploration and self-discovery. Fantasies often reveal aspects of ourselves that we may not fully understand or acknowledge. They shine a light on the parts of our psyche that crave attention, whether it's a longing for power, intimacy, creativity, or validation. For instance, a person who fantasizes about being in the spotlight might be uncovering a hidden desire for recognition, while someone who dreams of solitude in a remote cabin might be grappling with the chaos of their current surroundings. In these moments, fantasy acts as a mirror, reflecting not just what we want but also why we want it.

Yet, the mind's ability to construct elaborate fantasies is a double-edged sword. While these imagined scenarios can inspire and motivate, they can also distort reality and fuel dissatisfaction. The gap between fantasy and reality is often vast, and the more vivid the fantasy, the more glaring the disparity can seem. For example, someone who constantly fantasizes about an idealized partner might find themselves disillusioned with real-world relationships, where imperfections and compromises are inevitable. Similarly, a person who dreams of a glamorous career might feel trapped in their current job, even if it provides stability and fulfillment. When the mind becomes overly consumed by fantasy, it risks creating a sense of perpetual longing that no reality can satisfy.

The seductive nature of fantasy is amplified by its emotional intensity. Unlike reality, which is often messy and unpredictable, fantasy is under complete control of the individual's imagination. Every detail can be tailored to evoke the desired emotional response, whether it's exhilaration, comfort, or desire. This emotional potency is why fantasies can feel so compelling—they provide an idealized version of what we seek, untainted by the compromises and complexities of real life. However, this same intensity can make it difficult to let go of fantasies, even when they prove to be unrealistic or counterproductive.

An important aspect of understanding the role of fantasy is recognizing its roots in both biology and psychology. The brain's reward system, driven by dopamine, plays a significant role in the allure of imagined scenarios. When we fantasize, the brain often releases dopamine in anticipation of the pleasure associated with the imagined outcome. This chemical response reinforces the act of fantasizing, making it feel rewarding even when the fantasy itself is unattainable. Psychologically, fantasy serves as a way to process emotions and rehearse potential outcomes. It allows the mind to experiment with different possibilities, testing how they might feel without committing to them in reality.

Despite its inherent subjectivity, fantasy is also shaped by external influences. Cultural narratives, media, and societal expectations play a significant role in the content of our fantasies. A person raised in a culture that glorifies wealth and success might fantasize about luxury and power, while someone exposed to stories of romance and passion might dream of an all-consuming love. These influences do not create fantasies out of thin air but rather amplify and shape the desires that already exist within us. They provide a framework within which the imagination operates, subtly guiding what we fantasize about and how we perceive those fantasies.

The intersection of fantasy and reality becomes particularly complex in the context of relationships. Romantic fantasies, for instance, can both enhance and undermine real-world connections. On one hand, they can serve as a source of inspiration, encouraging individuals to pursue deeper intimacy and connection. On the other hand, they can create unrealistic expectations that no partner could ever fulfill. A person who idealizes their partner in their fantasies might struggle to reconcile this image with the partner's real-world flaws and limitations. Similarly, someone who fantasizes about a different kind of relationship might find themselves dissatisfied with their current one, even if it is otherwise healthy and fulfilling. Balancing the imaginative allure of fantasy with the grounded realities of relationships is a delicate but essential task.

Fantasy also plays a role in personal ambition and goal-setting. Imagining a desired future can be a powerful motivator, providing the vision and drive needed to overcome obstacles. A person who fantasizes about achieving a specific goal—whether it's writing a book, starting a business, or traveling the world—might use that mental image as fuel to take concrete steps toward making it a reality. However, the effectiveness of this approach depends on the individual's ability to distinguish between fantasy and action. While dreaming about a goal can be inspiring, it is the tangible efforts and sacrifices that bring it to fruition. When the mind becomes too engrossed in the fantasy, it risks substituting imagination for action, leaving the goal perpetually out of reach.

To harness the power of fantasy without becoming trapped by it, self-awareness is key. Understanding the role that fantasy plays in one's life—whether as a source of inspiration, escapism, or self-discovery—can help individuals navigate its complexities. Reflecting on the content and frequency of fantasies can provide valuable insights into unmet needs and desires, offering a roadmap for personal growth. For instance, someone who frequently fantasizes about adventure might consider incorporating more spontaneity and exploration into their daily life, while someone who dreams of recognition might focus on building confidence and pursuing opportunities to showcase their talents.

The mind's capacity for fantasy is a gift, but like any gift, it must be used wisely. When wielded with intention, fantasy can be a source of joy, creativity, and motivation. It can help individuals envision new possibilities, process their emotions, and connect with their innermost desires. However, when left unchecked, it can become an escape from reality, fostering dissatisfaction and perpetuating longing. The challenge lies in finding balance—embracing the imaginative freedom of fantasy while remaining grounded in the realities of the present.

When Cravings Collide with Reality

Cravings exist as powerful forces within us, often simmering beneath the surface, waiting for moments to rise and take hold of our actions, our thoughts, and even our decisions. They are deeply rooted in our psyche and biology, often stemming from unmet needs, repressed desires, or fleeting impulses. Cravings can be as simple as the urge to reach for a piece of chocolate or as complex as the longing for a life change—a new career, a romantic relationship, or a sense of freedom. But what happens when these cravings collide with the gritty, unyielding nature of reality? When the ideal in our minds clashes with the limitations and truths of the world around us, the result is often a profound struggle that can shape who we are and how we choose to move forward.

At their core, cravings are manifestations of desire. They are the whispers of what we think might bring us happiness, fulfillment, or relief. But these whispers are not always grounded in logic or practicality. Cravings are often impulsive, driven by the emotional and primitive parts of the brain, particularly the limbic system. This system, responsible for processing emotions and memories, can override rational thought when a craving becomes overpowering. For instance, the sudden, uncontrollable need to purchase something expensive may stem not from necessity but from a desire to fill an emotional void—perhaps boredom, loneliness, or a need for validation. The problem arises when that purchase leads to financial strain, creating a tension between the fleeting satisfaction of the craving and the long-term consequences of indulging it.

Reality, unlike craving, is unrelenting in its boundaries. It is shaped by external factors—time, resources, obligations, and the limitations of the physical world. Reality does not bend to the will of a craving, no matter how powerful the longing may feel. This collision between the two forces often creates an internal conflict, a tug-of-war between the immediate gratification we yearn for and the practical considerations that demand our attention. It's a common scenario: the temptation to devour an entire cake versus the reality of health goals, the urge to quit a stable job for a dream pursuit versus the weight of financial responsibilities, the desire for a passionate, all-consuming romance versus the realities of compromise and emotional labor in relationships.

The tension between craving and reality is not inherently negative. It is, in fact, a space of immense growth and self-reflection. When cravings collide with the constraints of reality, they force us to evaluate what truly matters. Is this desire worth pursuing? Is the craving genuine, or is it masking something deeper? And, most importantly, can a balance be struck between what we want and what is realistically achievable? These questions are not always easy to answer, but they are essential for navigating the complexities of human desire.

One of the key challenges in managing cravings is distinguishing between short-term impulses and long-term aspirations. Cravings often masquerade as urgent needs, demanding immediate attention and action. But not all cravings are created equal. Some are fleeting, triggered by a specific moment or environment, while others are more enduring, rooted in deeper desires or values. For example, the craving to binge-watch a television series might be a response to stress or fatigue, offering a temporary escape. On the other hand, the craving to travel the world might reflect a deeper longing for growth, adventure, and self-discovery. Recognizing the difference between these types of cravings allows us to prioritize and make decisions that align with our true goals.

When cravings meet the resistance of reality, the emotional response can often be frustration, disappointment, or even guilt. This is especially true when the craving feels tied to our identity or sense of self-worth. For instance, someone who craves artistic expression but feels stuck in a corporate job may grapple with feelings of inadequacy or failure. Similarly, a person yearning for a romantic connection but facing repeated rejections might internalize these experiences as a reflection of their own value. These emotional responses, while natural, can become barriers to understanding and addressing the root causes of the cravings.

The collision of cravings and reality also exposes the role of external influences in shaping our desires. Society, culture, and media often play a significant role in creating and amplifying cravings. Advertisements, for example, are designed to tap into our emotional triggers, convincing us that a product or service will fulfill our deepest needs. Social media platforms amplify this effect, presenting curated images of lifestyles, relationships, and achievements that seem tantalizingly within reach yet remain elusive. These external pressures can distort our understanding of what we truly want versus what we've been conditioned to believe we should want. When reality fails to align with these manufactured desires, it can lead to feelings of inadequacy, resentment, and a constant cycle of longing.

Navigating the space where cravings and reality intersect requires a combination of self-awareness, resilience, and intentionality. Self-awareness involves recognizing the source of a craving and understanding the emotions or needs driving it. Is the craving a response to a genuine desire, or is it a reaction to stress, boredom, or comparison? Resilience comes into play when reality imposes limits on our cravings. It's the ability to accept these limits without succumbing to despair, finding creative ways to adapt and pursue fulfillment within those boundaries. Intentionality, meanwhile, involves making conscious choices that align with our values and long-term goals rather than being swept away by the immediacy of a craving.

One effective strategy for managing the collision of cravings and reality is to reframe the narrative. Instead of viewing reality as an obstacle to desire, it can be seen as a tool for clarifying and refining what truly matters. The constraints of reality force us to be resourceful, to prioritize, and to let go of superficial or fleeting desires in favor of those that bring lasting satisfaction. For example, someone craving financial independence might initially feel frustrated by the limitations of their current circumstances. However, by reframing these constraints as an opportunity to develop discipline, creativity, and strategic thinking, they can channel their craving into actionable steps that bring them closer to their goal.

Another approach is to cultivate a sense of gratitude for the present moment, even when it falls short of our cravings. While it's natural to aspire for more, it's equally important to acknowledge and appreciate what we already have. This balance between ambition and contentment allows us to navigate the tension between craving and reality with grace and perspective. For instance, someone longing for a larger home might find fulfillment in creating a cozy, welcoming space within their current living situation, focusing on the aspects of their life that bring joy and connection.

Chapter 2: The Power Struggle Between Heart and Mind

Logic vs Emotion The Eternal Tug of War

The tension between logic and emotion is one of the most enduring and intricate struggles of the human experience. These two forces, seemingly at odds, govern our decisions, relationships, and the way we navigate the complexities of life. Logic, with its foundation in reason and structure, appeals to the rational mind, offering clarity and predictability. Emotion, on the other hand, emerges from the depths of our being, colored by feelings, instincts, and desires. The interplay between these two—one tethered to objectivity and the other to subjectivity— creates a dynamic push and pull that shapes our perceptions and choices, often in ways we don't fully recognize.

Throughout history, logic has been revered as the hallmark of human intelligence and progress. It is the tool we use to analyze problems, construct arguments, and make reasoned decisions. Logic provides a framework of consistency, a way to assess situations without being clouded by the volatility of emotions. It's what allows us to step back and weigh options, to predict outcomes based on evidence rather than impulse. It tells us, for instance, to save money for the future rather than indulging in every fleeting whim, to pause and gather facts before making a major life decision, or to consider the broader implications of our actions instead of focusing solely on immediate gratification. Logic is the voice in our minds that insists on balance, structure, and long-term thinking.

Yet, as compelling as logic may be, it cannot exist in isolation. Emotion, the counterweight to reason, is the force that gives life its vibrancy and meaning. Emotions drive our passions, motivate our actions, and connect us to others. They are the spark behind creativity, the foundation of empathy, and the source of resilience in the face of adversity. A purely logical approach to life, devoid of emotional influence, risks becoming cold, detached, and devoid of purpose. After all, it is emotion that compels us to pursue dreams, to fall in love, and to fight for causes we believe in. Without emotion, logic becomes a sterile exercise, a calculation without context or depth.

The tug of war between these two forces often manifests in our decision-making processes. Consider a scenario where someone is offered a high-paying job in a city far from their family and friends. Logic might dictate accepting the offer, pointing to financial stability, career progression, and long-term benefits. Emotion, however, may resist, highlighting the sadness of leaving loved ones behind and the fear of starting over in an unfamiliar place. Both perspectives are valid, yet they pull the individual in opposite directions, creating an internal struggle that can be difficult to resolve. This is the essence of the conflict between logic and emotion: the need to reconcile what makes sense with what feels right.

The workplace is another arena where this conflict often plays out. Managers, for instance, may find themselves torn between making decisions that are logically sound and those that take into account the emotional well-being of their team. A purely logic-driven leader might prioritize efficiency and results, enforcing strict policies without regard for how they affect morale. Conversely, a leader swayed entirely by emotion might struggle to make tough decisions, avoiding necessary but difficult conversations to spare feelings. The most effective leaders, then, are those who can strike a balance—using logic to guide their strategies while allowing emotion to inform their empathy and understanding.

Relationships, perhaps more than any other aspect of life, lay bare the tension between logic and emotion. Love, by its very nature, is deeply emotional, often defying rationality. People fall in love with individuals who may not align with their logical ideals, drawn instead by chemistry, connection, or shared experiences. Yet, sustaining a relationship requires a degree of logic—communication, compromise, and a mutual understanding of goals and values. A relationship built solely on emotion may burn brightly but struggle to endure, while one governed entirely by logic risks becoming transactional and devoid of passion. The healthiest relationships are those that embrace both dimensions, where emotion fuels connection and logic provides stability.

The clash between logic and emotion is not limited to personal decisions or relationships; it also extends to societal and cultural dynamics. Public debates on issues such as climate change, healthcare, and education often reveal the divide between logical analysis and emotional appeals. Logical arguments rely on data, evidence, and policy frameworks, while emotional appeals tap into fear, hope, and moral conviction. Both approaches have their strengths and limitations. Logical arguments may fail to resonate if they lack an emotional connection, while purely emotional rhetoric can oversimplify complex issues. Bridging this divide requires acknowledging the role of both forces and finding ways to integrate them into a coherent narrative.

One of the reasons this tension persists is that logic and emotion are rooted in different parts of the brain. Logic primarily engages the prefrontal cortex, responsible for reasoning, planning, and decision-making. Emotion, on the other hand, is driven by the limbic system, particularly the amygdala, which processes feelings such as fear, joy, and anger. These systems evolved to serve different purposes—logic to navigate external challenges and emotion to respond to internal and social cues. While they are interconnected, their differing functions can create conflict, particularly in situations that demand both rationality and emotional awareness.

Understanding this dynamic can help individuals navigate the tension more effectively. Rather than viewing logic and emotion as opposing forces, it is more productive to see them as complementary. Each has its strengths and weaknesses, and each can inform the other in meaningful ways. Logic can provide structure and clarity to emotional impulses, ensuring that decisions are thoughtful rather than reactive. Emotion, in turn, can humanize logic, grounding it in values, intuition, and a sense of purpose. When the two are in harmony, they create a balanced approach to life that is both rational and deeply connected.

Achieving this balance requires self-awareness and practice. It begins with recognizing when logic or emotion is dominating a situation and consciously inviting the other perspective into the conversation. For example, in moments of emotional upheaval, taking a step back to analyze the situation logically can provide much-needed perspective. Conversely, in moments of rigid rationality, allowing oneself to feel and empathize can lead to more compassionate and holistic decisions. This process is not about suppressing one force in favor of the other but about integrating them in a way that honors both.

The Rational Minds Retreat When Emotions Win

When emotions take over, the rational mind often retreats into the shadows, overwhelmed by the intensity of feelings that demand immediate attention. In these moments, logic and reason, typically our most trusted allies in decision-making, are sidelined, leaving emotions to dominate the stage. This phenomenon is not a failure of the mind but rather an inherent aspect of human nature. It is a reflection of how deeply intertwined our emotions are with our survival instincts, history, and sense of identity. The rational mind, for all its precision and clarity, is simply not equipped to compete with the immediacy and raw power of emotions when they surge to the forefront.

Emotions are primal. They originate in the most ancient parts of the brain, such as the amygdala, which evolved to process feelings swiftly and instinctively. This mechanism once served a critical purpose: fear alerted our ancestors to predators, anger fueled the fight for survival, and joy reinforced behaviors that ensured community and connection. These emotional responses were not just reactions; they were tools for survival, hardwired to override slower, more deliberate rational thought when urgency was required. Today, however, the threats we face are rarely life-or-death situations, and yet the brain's emotional circuitry remains just as reactive. A heated argument, a crushing disappointment, or even an unexpected failure can trigger this same cascade of emotional dominance.

When the rational mind retreats, decisions are often made in the heat of the moment. Anger, for example, might push someone to say something they later regret, words that cut deep and leave lasting scars. Fear might paralyze someone, preventing them from seizing an opportunity that could have changed their life. Even joy, when unchecked, might lead to overindulgence or reckless abandon, with little thought about the consequences. These decisions are not reflective of who we are at our core but are instead shaped by emotions that demand immediate resolution, often at the expense of long-term perspective.

One of the most compelling aspects of emotional dominance is its ability to distort perception. Emotions color how we interpret events, often exaggerating their significance or skewing their meaning. A simple critique from a colleague might feel like a personal attack under the weight of insecurity or frustration. A minor setback can feel like a monumental failure when amplified by self-doubt or anxiety. On the flip side, emotions can also blind us to potential risks. The euphoria of falling in love, for instance, might lead someone to overlook red flags in a relationship, rationalizing away concerns in favor of preserving the emotional high. In these moments, the rational mind doesn't disappear entirely—it simply fails to be heard over the noise of emotions clamoring for attention.

The retreat of rationality in the face of emotion is not always destructive; it can also lead to moments of profound authenticity and vulnerability. When emotions take the lead, they strip away the layers of pretense and calculation that often govern our interactions. A heartfelt apology, born from genuine remorse, carries a weight that no carefully worded logical explanation could match. A spontaneous act of kindness, driven by compassion, can create connections that logic alone would never inspire. Even tears, often viewed as a sign of weakness, can be a powerful expression of humanity, breaking down barriers and fostering understanding. These moments, raw and unfiltered, remind us that emotions are not inherently the enemy of rationality— they are its complement, adding depth and richness to the human experience.

However, the dominance of emotions can become problematic when it persists unchecked. Chronic emotional reactivity can lead to patterns of behavior that undermine well-being and relationships. A person who frequently lashes out in anger might alienate those they care about, creating a cycle of isolation and resentment. Someone who regularly succumbs to fear might find themselves trapped in a life of missed opportunities, unable to take the risks necessary for growth. Even positive emotions, when left unchecked, can have unintended consequences. Excessive optimism, for instance, might lead someone to ignore potential pitfalls or overcommit to unrealistic goals, resulting in eventual disappointment and burnout.

Understanding why the rational mind retreats when emotions win requires a closer look at the interplay between these two forces. Rationality relies on cognitive processes that are deliberate, analytical, and often slow. It takes time to gather information, weigh options, and consider outcomes. Emotions, by contrast, operate on a different timeline. They are immediate, visceral, and often unconscious, bypassing the slower pathways of rational thought to deliver an instant response. This speed is both a strength and a weakness. It allows emotions to act as an early warning system, alerting us to potential dangers or opportunities. But it also means they can outpace rationality, leading us to act before we've had a chance to think.

Managing the interplay between emotion and rationality is not about suppressing feelings or striving for perpetual calm. It's about cultivating an awareness of when emotions are taking over and learning how to create space for the rational mind to reassert itself. This begins with recognizing the physical and mental signs of emotional dominance: a racing heart, clenched fists, a flood of thoughts that feel urgent and overwhelming. These signals are the brain's way of alerting us to the rising tide of emotion. By acknowledging them without judgment, we can create a moment of pause—a space where rationality can reenter the equation.

One of the most effective ways to navigate emotional dominance is through grounding techniques. These techniques, which can include deep breathing, mindfulness, or even something as simple as counting to ten, help to calm the body's physiological response to emotion. By slowing the heart rate and reducing the flood of stress hormones, grounding creates the conditions necessary for the rational mind to regain its footing. It's not about eliminating the emotion but rather creating a balance where both emotion and reason have a voice.

Another key strategy is reframing—the practice of viewing a situation from multiple perspectives. When emotions dominate, they often narrow our focus, creating a tunnel vision that excludes alternative viewpoints. Reframing encourages us to step back and consider other interpretations of the event. For example, instead of seeing a failure as a definitive judgment of our worth, we might view it as a learning opportunity, a stepping stone toward growth. This shift in perspective doesn't diminish the emotional impact of the experience, but it tempers it with a dose of rationality, allowing for a more balanced response.

Over time, building emotional intelligence can strengthen the partnership between emotion and rationality. Emotional intelligence involves not only recognizing and understanding our own emotions but also navigating them in a way that aligns with our values and goals. It's about using emotions as information rather than letting them dictate our actions. A person with high emotional intelligence might feel anger rising in a conflict but choose to channel that energy into assertive communication rather than aggression. They might feel fear before a big decision but use that fear as a signal to prepare thoroughly rather than avoid the challenge altogether.

The Impulsive Heart Acting Without Thinking

Impulsivity is a double-edged sword. It is a force that can sweep us into action without hesitation, often bypassing the deliberations of the mind in favor of immediate gratification or response. At its core, impulsivity is driven by the heart—a restless, emotional engine that seeks to fulfill desires, avoid discomfort, or react to the stimulus of the moment. While there are times when acting on impulse can lead to spontaneity, creativity, or even serendipitous outcomes, the impulsive heart, unchecked and untempered by thought, can also steer us into treacherous waters. Acting without thinking often results in consequences we only recognize in hindsight, leaving us to wonder why we allowed emotion to take the wheel.

To understand impulsivity, it's important to recognize its biological underpinnings. The brain's reward system plays a significant role in driving impulsive behavior. The release of dopamine—a neurotransmitter associated with pleasure and satisfaction—occurs when we anticipate or achieve something desirable. When the heart yearns for instant gratification, the brain's reward system reinforces that urge, pushing us toward action without the pause required for critical thinking. This might explain why someone reaches for a sugary snack despite their commitment to a diet or why they hit "buy now" on an expensive item that wasn't in their budget. The impulsive heart seeks the dopamine rush, often at the expense of long-term considerations.

Impulsivity often thrives in moments of heightened emotion. Anger can ignite rash decisions as words fly out unchecked, leaving damage that can't easily be repaired. Excitement can lead to overcommitment, agreeing to plans or responsibilities without considering whether they're realistic. Fear might compel someone to flee a situation prematurely or seek comfort in unhealthy coping mechanisms. Even joy, in its exuberance, can blind us to potential repercussions. For example, the thrill of meeting someone new might lead to oversharing personal details or rushing into a relationship without fully understanding the other person's intentions. These moments are not inherently malicious or thoughtless; they are simply instances where the heart's emotional intensity overrides the mind's ability to analyze.

One of the most striking aspects of impulsivity is its ability to make us feel as though the decision we're about to make is not only necessary but urgent. The impulsive heart creates an illusion of immediacy, convincing us that the action we're driven to take cannot wait. This sense of urgency often shuts down the rational mind's attempts to weigh options or foresee outcomes. In reality, most decisions do not require instant action. However, the heart's impulsive nature thrives on the false belief that hesitation equals loss—of opportunity, satisfaction, or relief. It's why someone might blurt out a confession in the heat of the moment or lash out in anger when a more measured response would serve them better.

Impulsivity is not limited to the realm of emotions; it is also shaped by external factors. The environment we inhabit plays a significant role in triggering impulsive behavior. Social settings, for instance, can amplify impulsivity, particularly when peer pressure or group dynamics come into play. Someone might find themselves acting out of character at a party, driven by the energy of the crowd rather than their own values or intentions. Similarly, the digital age has created an ecosystem that nurtures impulsivity. Social media platforms, with their endless scroll of curated content, are designed to capture attention and provoke immediate reactions. The impulsive heart may lead someone to post a heated comment, make an unnecessary purchase, or compare themselves to others without considering the impact on their mental well-being.

The consequences of acting without thinking can vary in severity, but they often share a common thread: regret. Regret is the rational mind's way of reflecting on the choices made under the influence of the impulsive heart. It's the sinking feeling that follows a decision made in haste, the realization that a different action—or inaction—might have led to a better outcome. Regret, while painful, can also be a powerful teacher. It forces us to confront the gap between our impulses and our values, urging us to grow and develop strategies for managing impulsive tendencies in the future.

Impulsivity is not inherently negative. When channeled constructively, it can lead to moments of courage, passion, and authenticity. Some of history's most daring achievements were born from impulsive decisions—the leap of faith that defied convention or the bold action that broke through barriers of fear and doubt. However, the difference between constructive impulsivity and destructive impulsivity lies in the context and the ability to recognize when the heart is acting in alignment with the mind, rather than in opposition to it. Constructive impulses are often rooted in intuition—a deeper, subconscious form of understanding that guides us in the absence of complete information. Destructive impulses, on the other hand, are reactive, driven by fleeting emotions rather than thoughtful consideration.

Learning to navigate the impulsive heart requires a blend of self-awareness and intentionality. The first step is recognizing the triggers that provoke impulsive behavior. These triggers might be emotional, such as stress or excitement, or environmental, such as social pressure or advertising. By identifying the patterns that lead to impulsivity, it becomes easier to anticipate and manage them. For instance, someone who tends to make impulsive purchases might notice that their behavior is triggered by feelings of boredom or insecurity. Armed with this awareness, they can create strategies to address the underlying emotions without resorting to impulsive spending.

Another key strategy is cultivating the habit of pausing before acting. The impulsive heart thrives on immediacy, but even a brief moment of reflection can disrupt its momentum. This pause creates space for the rational mind to re-enter the conversation, offering perspective and clarity. Techniques such as deep breathing, counting to ten, or stepping away from the situation can help create this pause. The goal is not to suppress the heart's impulses but to allow the mind to join forces with the heart, ensuring that decisions are both emotionally and logically sound.

Setting boundaries can also be an effective way to manage impulsivity. Boundaries act as guardrails, preventing the impulsive heart from veering too far off course. These boundaries might be financial, such as setting a budget and sticking to it, or personal, such as limiting exposure to situations or environments that exacerbate impulsive tendencies. By establishing clear guidelines, it becomes easier to recognize when the heart's impulses are leading us astray and to course-correct before consequences escalate.

Over time, the relationship between the impulsive heart and the rational mind can become one of collaboration rather than conflict. The heart's impulses, when tempered by the mind's reason, can lead to decisions that are both bold and thoughtful, passionate and purposeful. This balance requires ongoing effort and self-reflection, but it is a skill that can be cultivated with practice. By embracing the impulses of the heart without letting them dictate our actions entirely, we can navigate life's challenges and opportunities with a sense of both authenticity and wisdom.

The Role of Past Experiences in Emotional Decisions

Past experiences shape the lens through which we view the world, deeply influencing the decisions we make, especially when emotions are involved. These experiences, etched into memory through repetition or intensity, create neural pathways that guide our reactions, often without conscious awareness. The choices we make when emotions are high are rarely isolated; they are colored and informed by the patterns, lessons, and wounds we've accumulated over time. The role of past experiences in emotional decisions is both profound and subtle, intertwining memory, emotion, and instinct in ways that often dictate our responses before logic has a chance to intervene.

The emotional weight of past experiences is stored primarily in the brain's limbic system, particularly in the amygdala and hippocampus. While the hippocampus catalogs events and contextual details, the amygdala assigns emotional significance to those memories. A breakup that shattered trust, a childhood moment of triumph, or the sting of a betrayal—all these experiences are stored not just as facts but as emotional imprints. When we face a situation that even vaguely resembles a past event, the amygdala works swiftly to bring those emotional memories to the surface, often bypassing rational thought. This is why someone who has been betrayed in the past might instinctively distrust others, even when there is no concrete evidence to warrant suspicion. It's not just the present moment they are responding to; it's the echoes of the past reverberating through their emotions.

These emotional imprints serve an evolutionary purpose. They act as a survival mechanism, helping us navigate a complex and often unpredictable world. A person who was once bitten by a dog might develop an instinctive fear of all dogs, an emotional decision intended to prevent future harm. Similarly, someone who experienced overwhelming support and love during a time of need may instinctively lean on others in moments of vulnerability, trusting in the goodness they've previously encountered. Emotions act as shortcuts for decision-making, drawing on past experiences to guide actions without requiring deliberate analysis. However, these shortcuts are not infallible; they can lead to overgeneralizations, misjudgments, and behaviors that may no longer serve us in our current context.

The influence of past experiences on emotional decisions can often be seen in patterns of behavior, particularly in relationships. A person who grew up in an environment where love was conditional might find themselves seeking approval in every interaction, fearing rejection even in situations where it's irrational. Conversely, someone who experienced consistent emotional neglect might struggle to form deep connections, instinctively withdrawing when faced with intimacy. These behaviors are not conscious choices but rather deeply ingrained emotional responses rooted in earlier experiences. They can feel automatic, as though the present situation demands a certain reaction, when in reality, it is the past dictating the terms.

Trauma, in particular, plays a significant role in shaping emotional decisions. Traumatic experiences leave deep psychological scars, often creating hypersensitivity to triggers that evoke memories of the original event. A victim of childhood bullying, for example, might react defensively to even mild criticism, interpreting it as an attack on their worth. These reactions are not proportional to the current situation but are amplified by the unresolved pain of the past. Trauma narrows the emotional bandwidth, making it difficult to differentiate between real threats and perceived ones. The body and mind, primed for self-protection, default to survival mode, bypassing rationality in favor of emotional reflex.

However, the impact of past experiences is not limited to negative or traumatic events. Positive experiences can also shape emotional decisions in powerful ways. A person who grew up in a nurturing environment might approach life with a sense of optimism and trust, making decisions that reflect their belief in the goodness of others. Similarly, someone who has experienced the rewards of taking risks—whether in their career, relationships, or personal growth—might be more inclined to make bold emotional decisions, trusting in their ability to navigate uncertainty. Positive experiences create a foundation of emotional resilience, allowing individuals to approach challenges with confidence and an open heart.

The challenge lies in recognizing when past experiences are influencing emotional decisions in ways that are no longer helpful. This requires a level of self-awareness that can be difficult to achieve, particularly in moments of heightened emotion. The mind's natural tendency is to react, not reflect, making it easy to fall into patterns that feel familiar, even if they are counterproductive. For instance, someone who has been hurt in past relationships might find themselves sabotaging new connections, pushing people away before they have the chance to get too close. This behavior, while rooted in self-protection, ultimately prevents the possibility of meaningful connection.

Self-awareness begins with identifying the emotional triggers that bring past experiences to the surface. Triggers are often subtle and may not immediately reveal their connection to earlier events. A casual comment from a coworker, a particular tone of voice, or even a smell can evoke strong emotional reactions that feel disproportionate to the current situation. By paying attention to these reactions and tracing them back to their origin, it becomes possible to disentangle the past from the present. For example, recognizing that an overwhelming fear of failure stems from a childhood marked by high expectations can help reframe current challenges as opportunities rather than threats.

Once triggers are identified, the next step is to challenge the assumptions and beliefs they reinforce. Past experiences, particularly negative ones, often create narratives that shape how we perceive ourselves and the world. These narratives can be limiting, convincing us that we are unworthy, incapable, or destined to repeat the same mistakes. Challenging these beliefs requires both courage and compassion. It involves questioning their validity and replacing them with narratives that reflect the reality of the present moment rather than the pain of the past. For instance, someone who believes they are unlovable because of a history of rejection might work to affirm their worthiness of love and connection, recognizing that the actions of others do not define their value.

Cultivating emotional intelligence is another powerful tool for navigating the influence of past experiences. Emotional intelligence involves not only recognizing and understanding one's emotions but also managing them in ways that align with one's values and goals. This includes developing the ability to pause before reacting, creating space for reflection and intentionality. By learning to observe emotions without immediately acting on them, it becomes possible to make decisions that are informed by both emotion and reason, rather than being driven solely by the past.

Forgiveness, both of oneself and others, can also play a transformative role in breaking free from the grip of past experiences. Holding onto anger, resentment, or regret ties us to the events that caused those emotions, allowing them to continue influencing our decisions. Forgiveness is not about condoning harmful behavior or minimizing pain; it is about releasing the hold that those experiences have on our emotional well-being. By forgiving, we reclaim the power to make decisions based on the present moment rather than the wounds of the past.

Breaking Free from Emotional Sabotage

Patterns of emotional sabotage often operate in the shadows of our consciousness, quietly dictating our actions and decisions. These patterns can manifest as self-doubt, procrastination, avoidance, or even destructive behaviors, all of which serve to undermine our goals, relationships, and personal growth. Emotional sabotage is not always deliberate; more often than not, it arises from internalized fears, unresolved wounds, and limiting beliefs. It acts as a defense mechanism, keeping us within the boundaries of comfort zones shaped by past pain or perceived inadequacies. Breaking free from emotional sabotage requires not only awareness but also deliberate, sustained effort to rewrite the scripts that hold us back.

One of the most insidious forms of emotional sabotage is self-doubt. It whispers falsehoods, telling us we are not good enough, capable enough, or deserving enough to succeed. This internal voice often originates from experiences of criticism, failure, or rejection, which leave a lasting impression on our sense of self-worth. Over time, these messages become ingrained, forming a narrative that dictates our actions. For instance, someone who was consistently told as a child that they were "not smart enough" might subconsciously avoid opportunities for growth, fearing that failure will only reinforce this belief. Self-doubt, when left unchecked, becomes a self-fulfilling prophecy, as the fear of inadequacy creates a cycle of avoidance and stagnation.

Procrastination is another common manifestation of emotional sabotage. On the surface, it may seem like mere laziness or poor time management, but beneath the surface often lies a deeper emotional struggle. Procrastination frequently stems from fear—fear of failure, fear of success, or even fear of the unknown. When faced with a daunting task or goal, the mind may seek refuge in distraction, convincing itself that there will always be more time. This delay, however, often leads to increased stress, diminished performance, and, ultimately, a sense of regret. The act of procrastination becomes a way to self-sabotage, allowing us to avoid confronting the emotions tied to the task at hand.

Avoidance behaviors take many forms, from sidestepping difficult conversations to steering clear of opportunities that challenge us. These behaviors are rooted in a desire to protect ourselves from discomfort, rejection, or potential pain. While avoidance can provide temporary relief, it often comes at a long-term cost. A person who avoids addressing conflict in a relationship, for example, may preserve peace in the short term but risks allowing resentment to fester, eroding the connection over time. Similarly, avoiding career opportunities out of fear of inadequacy can lead to feelings of unfulfilled potential. Avoidance, like other forms of emotional sabotage, often reinforces the very fears it seeks to mitigate, creating a cycle of self-limitation.

Destructive behaviors, such as overindulgence, reckless decisions, or unhealthy coping mechanisms, are perhaps the most overt forms of emotional sabotage. These behaviors often serve as a way to numb or escape from difficult emotions, providing temporary relief at the expense of long-term well-being. For instance, someone who feels overwhelmed by stress might turn to excessive alcohol consumption as a way to cope, only to find that it exacerbates their problems. Destructive behaviors are often driven by a lack of emotional regulation, as unresolved feelings build up until they demand release in ways that are ultimately harmful. Breaking free from these behaviors requires not only addressing the symptoms but also confronting the underlying emotional triggers.

The first step in overcoming emotional sabotage is cultivating self-awareness. It is impossible to change what we do not recognize. Developing a habit of introspection can help identify the patterns and triggers that contribute to self-sabotaging behaviors. This process might involve journaling, mindfulness practices, or even therapy to uncover the roots of these patterns. For instance, someone who struggles with procrastination might notice that their avoidance is most pronounced when they feel unprepared or fear judgment. By identifying these triggers, they can begin to address the underlying emotions rather than simply focusing on the behavior itself.

Challenging limiting beliefs is another crucial aspect of breaking free from emotional sabotage. These beliefs often operate as unquestioned truths, shaping our perceptions and decisions without our conscious awareness. To challenge them, it is necessary to examine their validity and replace them with more empowering narratives. For example, a belief like "I'm not good enough to succeed" can be countered with evidence of past accomplishments or affirmations that emphasize growth and effort over perfection. Rewriting these internal scripts takes time and practice, but it is essential for dismantling the foundations of self-sabotage.

Learning to sit with discomfort is also key to overcoming emotional sabotage. Many self-sabotaging behaviors arise from an aversion to uncomfortable emotions, such as fear, sadness, or vulnerability. However, avoiding these emotions only strengthens their hold over us. By allowing ourselves to feel and process these emotions, we can begin to break their power. This might involve acknowledging the fear of failure rather than avoiding it, or expressing sadness rather than suppressing it. Emotional resilience grows when we confront our feelings head-on, rather than seeking to escape them through sabotage.

Setting realistic goals and boundaries can help create a framework for success that minimizes opportunities for self-sabotage. Unrealistic expectations often set the stage for failure, reinforcing feelings of inadequacy and perpetuating the cycle of sabotage. By setting achievable goals and breaking them into manageable steps, we create a sense of progress and accomplishment that counters self-doubt. Similarly, establishing boundaries—whether with others or with ourselves—can prevent situations that trigger self-sabotaging behaviors. For instance, setting limits on work hours can reduce burnout, while saying no to unnecessary commitments can create space for self-care and focus.

Accountability can also play a powerful role in overcoming emotional sabotage. Sharing goals and challenges with a trusted friend, mentor, or therapist creates a sense of responsibility and support. External accountability can provide motivation and perspective, helping to counteract the internal voices of doubt or avoidance. For example, someone who struggles with procrastination might benefit from setting deadlines with a colleague or enlisting a friend to check in on their progress. Accountability fosters a sense of connection and encouragement, making it easier to stay on track.

Self-compassion is perhaps the most important tool in breaking free from emotional sabotage. Many self-sabotaging behaviors are fueled by harsh self-criticism, which creates a cycle of shame and avoidance. Practicing self-compassion involves treating oneself with kindness and understanding, particularly in moments of failure or struggle. It means recognizing that imperfection is part of the human experience and that mistakes are opportunities for growth rather than evidence of inadequacy. By cultivating self-compassion, we create a supportive internal environment that encourages progress rather than perpetuating sabotage.

Breaking free from emotional sabotage is not a one-time effort but an ongoing journey. It requires patience, persistence, and a willingness to confront the uncomfortable truths that lie beneath our behaviors. Along the way, setbacks are inevitable, but they are also opportunities to learn and grow. Each step forward, no matter how small, represents a victory over the patterns that once held us back. Over time, as self-awareness deepens and new habits take root, the grip of e

Chapter 3: The Breaking Point of Desire

Recognizing the Edge When Desire Becomes All Consuming

Desire is a powerful force that drives much of human behavior. It fuels ambition, sparks creativity, and propels us toward our goals. Yet, like a flame, it must be tended carefully. When left unchecked, desire can grow uncontrollably, consuming everything in its path and leaving us feeling hollow, unfulfilled, or even lost. Recognizing the edge—the point where healthy aspiration shifts into an all-consuming obsession—is critical for maintaining balance and preserving emotional well-being. The line is often subtle, blurred by the intensity of our wants and the societal glorification of relentlessness. Learning to identify this edge is not about suppressing desire but about understanding its boundaries and ensuring it serves rather than controls us.

Desire begins with a spark, often ignited by a yearning for something we believe will enhance our lives. It could be the pursuit of a career milestone, a romantic connection, material wealth, or personal achievement. At its best, desire motivates us to grow, take risks, and push beyond our comfort zones. It fuels resilience, giving us the courage to endure setbacks and continue striving toward our aspirations. This kind of balanced desire is productive—it aligns with our values, respects our limits, and leaves room for the other facets of our lives to thrive.

However, desire has a way of growing insatiable, particularly when it becomes entangled with validation, fear, or unmet emotional needs. The career milestone morphs into an endless chase for recognition. The pursuit of wealth transforms into a compulsive quest for accumulation, far beyond what is necessary or meaningful. The longing for love or connection becomes a desperate fixation, overshadowing self-worth or mutual respect. When desire becomes all-consuming, it stops being a force for growth and starts eroding the very foundation of our emotional and mental health. It narrows focus to the point where nothing else seems to matter, creating an imbalance that can lead to burnout, frustration, or disillusionment.

One of the warning signs that desire is becoming all-consuming is a loss of perspective. When the object of our desire takes precedence over everything else—our relationships, our health, our integrity—it is a clear indication that we are nearing the edge. For instance, someone striving for professional success might start neglecting their family, sacrificing meaningful connections for the sake of climbing the corporate ladder. The initial motivation to provide for loved ones or achieve personal fulfillment becomes overshadowed by an unrelenting need to prove oneself or maintain a certain image. This tunnel vision not only affects the individual but also ripples outward, impacting those around them.

Another indicator is the inability to experience satisfaction, even after achieving milestones. When desire becomes all-consuming, it often brings with it a sense of perpetual inadequacy. No matter how much we accomplish, it never feels like enough. The goalposts keep moving, and the gratification we once anticipated becomes fleeting or nonexistent. This is because all-consuming desire shifts the focus from the journey to an endless fixation on the destination—one that, paradoxically, always seems just out of reach. The joy of progress, the lessons learned along the way, and the connections formed during the pursuit are overshadowed by the relentless drive for more.

The physical and emotional toll of unchecked desire can also reveal its consuming nature. Stress, exhaustion, and anxiety are common companions of those who push themselves beyond their limits in pursuit of their wants. The body and mind send warning signals—insomnia, irritability, chronic fatigue—but these are often ignored in the name of ambition or necessity. Over time, these symptoms compound, leading to burnout, diminished productivity, and even health problems. The irony is that the very drive meant to improve our lives ends up depleting us, leaving us with little energy or capacity to enjoy the fruits of our labor.

Social and cultural influences often exacerbate the risk of desire becoming all-consuming. In a world that glorifies hustle culture and equates self-worth with achievement, it's easy to fall into the trap of believing that more is always better. Social media amplifies this pressure, showcasing curated images of success, wealth, and happiness that create unrealistic expectations. The comparison game takes root, feeding a cycle of envy and inadequacy that fuels relentless striving. This external validation can become addictive, driving us further away from intrinsic motivation and deeper into the grip of all-consuming desire.

Recognizing the edge requires a willingness to pause and reflect. Self-awareness is the first step in understanding whether our desires are serving us or controlling us. This involves asking difficult questions: Why do I want this? What am I hoping to achieve or feel? Am I sacrificing things that truly matter in pursuit of this goal? Honest answers can reveal whether our desires align with our values or whether they have veered into unhealthy territory. For instance, someone chasing financial success might realize that their true motivation is a fear of scarcity rooted in childhood experiences, rather than a genuine need for more wealth.

Setting boundaries is essential for maintaining balance. These boundaries can take many forms, from limiting the time and energy devoted to a particular pursuit to establishing clear priorities that honor the full spectrum of one's life. For example, a person striving for career advancement might set a boundary to avoid working weekends, ensuring time for family, hobbies, or self-care. Boundaries act as guardrails, preventing desire from consuming every aspect of our lives.

Cultivating gratitude can also help temper the intensity of desire. When we focus on what we already have, rather than fixating on what we lack, it becomes easier to appreciate the present moment. Gratitude shifts the perspective from scarcity to abundance, reducing the compulsive need to chase more. This doesn't mean abandoning ambition but rather approaching it from a place of contentment and self-assurance. A person who practices gratitude might still strive for professional success, but they do so with the understanding that their worth is not defined solely by their achievements.

Mindfulness is another valuable tool for recognizing and managing the edge of all-consuming desire. By cultivating a practice of present-moment awareness, we can observe our thoughts and emotions without becoming entangled in them. This allows us to notice when desire begins to dominate our thinking or behavior, creating space to choose a more balanced response. For instance, someone feeling overwhelmed by the need to accomplish a goal might use mindfulness techniques to ground themselves, reconnecting with their values and priorities.

It is also important to redefine success on our own terms. When desire becomes all-consuming, it is often because we have adopted external measures of success rather than defining what truly matters to us. Taking the time to reflect on personal values and aspirations can help clarify what we genuinely want, rather than what we feel pressured to want. This might involve shifting focus from material wealth to meaningful relationships, from public recognition to personal fulfillment, or from relentless striving to sustainable growth.

Breaking free from the grip of all-consuming desire is not about extinguishing ambition or rejecting the pursuit of goals. It is about creating harmony between aspiration and contentment, ensuring that our desires enhance rather than detract from our lives. By recognizing the edge and stepping back when necessary, we can cultivate a sense of balance that allows us to pursue our dreams without losing ourselves in the process. Desire, when tempered with self-awareness and intention, becomes a powerful ally rather than an oppressive force.

Obsession vs Passion Knowing the Difference

The line between obsession and passion is as fine as it is crucial. Both are driven by an intense focus and commitment, yet they reside in vastly different emotional territories. Passion is invigorating, life-affirming, and constructive, while obsession often spirals into a consuming force that narrows perspective, distorts priorities, and can even harm mental health and relationships. These two forces, though they might appear similar on the surface, diverge in their impact on our well-being and the way they guide our actions. Understanding this distinction is essential for harnessing the power of passion without falling into the destructive grip of obsession.

Passion originates from a place of genuine interest and love for something. It's the spark that makes you stay up late perfecting a craft, the energy that drives you to learn and grow, or the enthusiasm that fuels your pursuit of goals. Passion fills you with a sense of purpose and joy, often leaving you feeling fulfilled even after hard work or setbacks. It is expansive, allowing space for other aspects of your life to coexist alongside it. Someone passionate about writing, for instance, may dedicate countless hours to their craft, but they also find balance by nurturing relationships, taking care of their health, and engaging in other interests. Passion is not just a commitment to the process but also an appreciation for the journey, embracing its ups and downs with a sense of curiosity and resilience.

Obsession, on the other hand, often masquerades as passion in its early stages. It begins with a similar intensity, but over time, it becomes all-consuming, narrowing focus to the point where everything else fades into insignificance. Unlike passion, which inspires and uplifts, obsession often breeds anxiety, frustration, and dissatisfaction. It is driven not just by a desire for success or achievement but by an underlying fear—fear of failure, fear of inadequacy, or fear of losing control. While passion welcomes challenges as opportunities for growth, obsession views them as threats that must be overcome at all costs, often leading to a destructive cycle of perfectionism and self-criticism.

One of the key differences lies in how the two impact your emotional state. Passion energizes and motivates, even when the work is challenging. It provides a sense of meaning and accomplishment, helping you to bounce back from setbacks with renewed determination. Obsession, however, drains energy and creates a constant undercurrent of stress. It often feels like a compulsion rather than a choice, leaving little room for joy or spontaneity. A person consumed by obsession might achieve impressive results in the short term, but the emotional toll can be significant, leading to burnout, strained relationships, and a diminished sense of self-worth.

The way passion and obsession influence relationships is another important distinction. Passion enhances connections by inspiring others and fostering collaboration. When someone is passionate about a cause or pursuit, their enthusiasm is often contagious, drawing others in and creating opportunities for shared experiences. Obsession, however, tends to isolate. It demands excessive time and attention, often at the expense of loved ones and social bonds. A person obsessed with their career, for example, might neglect family and friends, prioritizing work above all else. Over time, this imbalance can lead to resentment, loneliness, and a sense of disconnection from the people who matter most.

Another way to differentiate between passion and obsession is by examining the role of control. Passion is inherently flexible; it adapts to circumstances and evolves over time. Someone passionate about art might explore different mediums or take breaks to recharge, trusting that their creative drive will remain intact. Obsession, however, is rigid and unyielding. It demands complete control and perfection, leaving little room for adaptability or imperfection. This need for control often stems from deeper insecurities, as the obsessive individual ties their self-worth to their ability to achieve specific outcomes. When things don't go as planned, the emotional fallout can be overwhelming, reinforcing the cycle of obsession.

Recognizing the difference between passion and obsession requires honest self-reflection. It's important to examine not just your actions but also the underlying motivations driving them. Ask yourself whether your pursuit brings you joy and fulfillment or whether it leaves you feeling anxious and depleted. Consider whether your focus enhances your life or whether it comes at the expense of other important aspects, such as relationships, health, or personal growth. Reflect on how you respond to setbacks: do they inspire you to learn and improve, or do they trigger a sense of panic and self-doubt? These questions can help illuminate whether your drive is rooted in passion or whether it has veered into the territory of obsession.

Creating balance is key to nurturing passion while avoiding obsession. This involves setting boundaries and maintaining perspective, ensuring that your pursuits remain a source of inspiration rather than a source of stress. One way to do this is by diversifying your interests and priorities. While it's natural to pour energy into something you're passionate about, it's also important to make time for other activities that bring you joy and fulfillment. This might include spending time with loved ones, exploring new hobbies, or simply taking time to rest and recharge. By creating a well-rounded life, you can prevent any one pursuit from becoming all-consuming.

Practicing self-compassion is another important tool for maintaining balance. Passion thrives in an environment of curiosity and kindness, where mistakes and setbacks are viewed as opportunities for growth rather than as failures. Obsession, however, often feeds on self-criticism and unrealistic expectations. By treating yourself with patience and understanding, you can create the emotional space needed to pursue your goals without succumbing to the pressures of perfectionism. This might involve setting realistic expectations, celebrating small victories, or simply reminding yourself that your worth is not defined by your achievements.

Mindfulness can also play a powerful role in distinguishing between passion and obsession. By cultivating awareness of your thoughts and emotions, you can better understand the motivations driving your actions and recognize when your focus becomes unbalanced. Mindfulness encourages you to stay present in the moment, appreciating the process rather than fixating solely on the outcome. This shift in perspective can help you stay grounded, allowing you to engage with your passions in a healthy and sustainable way.

Ultimately, the difference between passion and obsession lies in their impact on your overall well-being. Passion enriches your life, fostering growth, connection, and fulfillment. It aligns with your values and supports a sense of purpose, leaving you energized and inspired. Obsession, in contrast, depletes your resources, narrowing your focus and creating a sense of imbalance. It often stems from fear or insecurity, leading to a cycle of stress and dissatisfaction. By recognizing these distinctions and cultivating a mindful, balanced approach to your pursuits, you can harness the power of passion without falling into the destructive patterns of obsession.

The Cost of Losing Control: When Desire Takes Over

When desire takes over, it often enters uninvited, slipping through the cracks of rationality and weaving itself into every corner of decision-making. At first, it might seem benign—an invigorating drive that pushes you to achieve or obtain what you crave. But beneath this intensity lies a hidden cost, one that often goes unnoticed until it begins to manifest in tangible and intangible ways. Losing control to desire can lead to consequences that ripple through every aspect of life, from compromised relationships to neglected self-care, from financial instability to a fractured sense of self. Understanding these costs is not about demonizing desire but about recognizing its capacity to overwhelm, distort priorities, and quietly dismantle the balance necessary for a fulfilling life.

Desire, by its nature, is seductive. It appeals to our emotional core, whispering promises of satisfaction, happiness, or validation just out of reach. The allure of something we deeply yearn for—a promotion, a romantic partner, material wealth, or even social recognition—can be so powerful that it overrides our better judgment. It becomes easy to justify questionable decisions or sacrifices, all in service of fulfilling that longing. But when desire begins to dictate behavior, it often comes at a price. The first casualty is usually perspective. The singular focus created by unchecked desire narrows the lens through which we view the world. Suddenly, everything revolves around the object of our longing, and other priorities fade into the background. Obligations are postponed, relationships are neglected, and self-care becomes an afterthought. The tunnel vision that emerges can feel intoxicating in its intensity, but it also blinds us to the broader context of our lives.

One of the most common costs of losing control to desire is the erosion of relationships. When desire takes precedence over everything else, the people around us often bear the brunt of our misplaced priorities. This can take many forms—cancelled plans, unreturned calls, or a growing distance in emotional availability. For example, someone consumed by the desire for professional success might spend long hours at the office, missing important family events or neglecting the small, everyday moments that nurture intimacy. Over time, these absences accumulate, creating a sense of disconnection and resentment. The irony is often bitter: the very relationships that could provide support and grounding during the pursuit of a goal are the ones most likely to suffer.

Another cost lies in the toll on personal well-being. When desire takes control, it often demands sacrifices that chip away at physical and mental health. Sleep is traded for late-night work sessions, meals are skipped in the rush to meet deadlines, and moments of rest are replaced with relentless activity. The body and mind, pushed beyond their limits, begin to signal distress through exhaustion, irritability, or even illness. Yet, in the grip of desire, these warnings are frequently ignored. The pursuit becomes all-encompassing, leaving little room for reflection or self-care. Over time, this neglect can lead to burnout—a state of emotional, physical, and mental depletion that makes it nearly impossible to continue the very pursuit that caused it.

Financial consequences are another potential cost of losing control to desire. This is particularly evident when the object of desire is tied to material aspirations—luxury goods, status symbols, or lifestyle upgrades. The craving for these items can lead to impulsive spending, debt accumulation, or financial instability. Take, for example, someone driven by the desire to project an image of success. They might purchase a car or wardrobe beyond their means, justifying the expense as necessary for maintaining appearances. But as the bills pile up and the stress of financial strain sets in, the fleeting satisfaction of those purchases reveals its hollowness. The cost of losing financial control extends beyond monetary loss; it undermines a sense of security and creates a lingering burden of anxiety.

Perhaps the most profound cost of losing control to desire is the impact on one's sense of self. When desire dictates actions, it often distorts identity, aligning it too closely with the pursuit of external validation or achievement. The person who once found joy in creative expression might now create solely to impress others. The individual who once sought career growth for personal fulfillment might now chase titles for the sake of status. In these moments, the intrinsic motivations that once defined a person become overshadowed by the need to meet external expectations or societal standards. This shift can lead to a loss of authenticity, as actions are no longer guided by internal values but by the relentless pull of desire.

The consequences of losing control to desire are not always immediate; they often unfold gradually, making them difficult to recognize in the moment. This slow erosion can create a false sense of security, as the initial pursuit of desire often yields results—promotions are earned, goals are met, and milestones are achieved. But the underlying costs accumulate quietly, revealing themselves only when the foundation begins to crack. The neglected relationships, compromised health, and diminished sense of self eventually come into sharp focus, creating a reckoning that is both painful and unavoidable.

Breaking free from the grip of overpowering desire requires a deliberate effort to regain control and restore balance. The first step is cultivating self-awareness—developing the ability to recognize when desire begins to dominate thoughts and actions. This involves paying attention to warning signs, such as growing impatience, irritability, or an inability to focus on anything other than the object of desire. Self-awareness also means reflecting on the motivations behind the pursuit: Is this something I truly want, or am I driven by fear, insecurity, or societal pressure? Am I sacrificing too much in the process? Honest answers to these questions can provide the clarity needed to step back and reassess priorities.

Establishing boundaries is another essential strategy for managing desire. Boundaries act as guardrails, preventing the pursuit of a goal from encroaching on other areas of life. This might involve setting limits on the time and energy devoted to a particular pursuit, ensuring that relationships, health, and personal growth are not neglected. For example, someone striving for professional success might commit to leaving work at a certain time each day, creating space for family, hobbies, or relaxation. By setting clear boundaries, it becomes easier to maintain balance and avoid the tunnel vision that unchecked desire can create.

Practicing gratitude can also help temper the intensity of desire. When we focus on what we already have, rather than fixating on what we lack, it becomes easier to appreciate the present moment and resist the urge to overreach. Gratitude shifts the perspective from scarcity to abundance, reducing the compulsion to chase more. This doesn't mean abandoning ambition but rather approaching it with a sense of contentment and groundedness. A person who practices gratitude might still strive for success, but they do so with the understanding that their worth is not defined solely by their achievements.

Mindfulness is another powerful tool for regaining control. By cultivating a practice of present-moment awareness, it becomes possible to observe the pull of desire without immediately acting on it. Mindfulness encourages a pause—a moment to reflect on whether the pursuit is truly worth the sacrifice it demands. This pause creates space for intentional decision-making, allowing actions to be guided by values rather than impulses. Over time, this practice can help build resilience against the seductive pull of desire, fostering a sense of balance and clarity.

Red Flags in the Pursuit of Longing

The pursuit of longing can be an exhilarating journey, filled with moments of discovery, ambition, and personal growth. Longing—whether it's for love, success, recognition, or fulfillment—has the power to propel individuals toward extraordinary achievements. It is often a reflection of our deepest desires and values, revealing what we yearn for most in life. However, there are moments when the pursuit of longing veers into dangerous territory. This is where red flags emerge, warning signs that the path you're on may be leading you away from fulfillment and toward harm. Ignoring these signals can result in emotional exhaustion, strained relationships, and a sense of being lost, rather than finding the satisfaction you sought.

One of the earliest red flags is a growing sense of disconnection. Longing, when pursued with balance and intention, often brings clarity and alignment with one's values. But when the pursuit becomes obsessive or misaligned, it creates a rift between who you are and who you are trying to become. This disconnection can manifest as a feeling of unease, as though the person you see in the mirror no longer resembles your authentic self. You might find yourself making compromises that clash with your principles, justifying actions that would have once felt unacceptable. For example, someone longing for professional success might start cutting corners or betraying their own ethics to achieve their goals, rationalizing these actions as necessary sacrifices. Over time, these small betrayals of self can accumulate, leaving you with a sense of alienation and regret.

Another red flag emerges when the pursuit begins to consume your life, leaving little room for anything else. Healthy longing inspires balance, encouraging you to grow in multiple areas of your life rather than fixating on one. When longing becomes all-consuming, however, it often leads to neglect—of relationships, hobbies, health, and even basic needs. You might notice that the people who once brought you joy now feel like distractions, or that activities you used to love no longer hold your interest. This narrowing of focus can create a dangerous feedback loop, where the more you invest in your longing, the more isolated you become, and the more isolated you become, the more you cling to the object of your longing as a source of meaning.

A third warning sign is the inability to find satisfaction, no matter how much progress you make. Longing, when pursued with a healthy mindset, is accompanied by moments of joy and accomplishment along the way. Each step forward feels like a small victory, reinforcing your sense of purpose. But when you find yourself constantly moving the goalposts—never content with what you've achieved—the pursuit begins to take on a different tone. This insatiable longing often stems from deeper emotional wounds, such as feelings of inadequacy or a fear of never being enough. No matter how much you accomplish, it never feels sufficient because the longing is no longer about the goal itself but about filling a void that external achievements cannot satisfy.

Another red flag is the erosion of boundaries. In a healthy pursuit, boundaries protect your well-being, ensuring that your longing remains a part of your life rather than taking over entirely. But when those boundaries begin to blur, it's a sign that the pursuit may have become unhealthy. You might find yourself saying yes to demands that overextend you, sacrificing sleep, health, or personal values to keep pushing forward. This overreach can lead to exhaustion and resentment, not only toward yourself but also toward the very goal you once cherished. For instance, someone longing for financial security might take on excessive work hours, ignoring their physical and mental limits, only to find that the stress outweighs any sense of accomplishment.

The strain on relationships is another critical red flag. Longing, when approached with balance, often enriches relationships, as it gives you a sense of purpose and fulfillment that you can share with others. But when the pursuit becomes unhealthy, it often creates distance and conflict. Loved ones may feel neglected, unimportant, or even resentful as your focus shifts entirely to your longing. They might voice their concerns, only to be met with defensiveness or denial. Over time, these strained dynamics can erode trust and intimacy, leaving you feeling isolated and unsupported. The irony is painful: the deeper your longing grows, the more it alienates the people who could provide the connection and grounding you need most.

Another red flag to watch for is a growing reliance on external validation. When longing is driven by an intrinsic sense of purpose, the journey itself is rewarding. But when it becomes tied to the approval or recognition of others, it can lead to a precarious dependence on external validation. You might find yourself constantly seeking praise, likes, or accolades, using them as a measure of your worth or progress.

This external focus not only diminishes your sense of autonomy but also makes you vulnerable to the opinions and judgments of others. The pursuit of longing becomes less about fulfilling your own aspirations and more about meeting the expectations of those around you, leaving you feeling unanchored and disconnected from your true self.

Physical and emotional symptoms often serve as another set of red flags. The body and mind are remarkably adept at signaling when something is amiss, but these signals are easy to overlook in the heat of pursuit. You might experience chronic fatigue, headaches, or insomnia, dismissing them as minor inconveniences rather than warnings. Emotionally, you might feel irritable, anxious, or overwhelmed, yet find it difficult to pinpoint the cause. These symptoms are often the result of prolonged stress and imbalance, as the relentless pursuit of longing takes a toll on your overall well-being. Ignoring these signals can lead to more serious consequences, from burnout to mental health struggles that require significant intervention.

A final red flag is the loss of joy and spontaneity. Longing, when pursued with a sense of balance and curiosity, often brings moments of playfulness and delight. But when the pursuit becomes rigid and compulsive, it leaves little room for joy. You might find that even activities you once enjoyed feel like obligations, weighed down by the pressure to perform or succeed. The spontaneity that once brought excitement to your life is replaced by a relentless drive to stick to a plan or achieve a specific outcome. Over time, this rigidity can drain the color and vibrancy from your days, leaving you feeling stuck in a monotonous cycle of striving without satisfaction.

Recognizing these red flags is an essential step in recalibrating your pursuit of longing. It requires self-awareness, honesty, and a willingness to pause and reflect. Ask yourself whether your longing is enhancing your life or depleting it. Are you finding joy and meaning in the journey, or are you consumed by stress and dissatisfaction? Are your relationships thriving, or are they suffering under the weight of your focus? These questions can help you identify when your pursuit has crossed into unhealthy territory and guide you toward making the changes needed to restore balance.

The Emotional Fallout of Unchecked Desire

Unchecked desire has a way of creeping into our emotional core, weaving itself into the fabric of our lives in ways that are often subtle at first but devastating over time. While desire itself is not inherently harmful—it is, after all, a natural and powerful motivator—it becomes dangerous when left unchecked, when it grows beyond its intended purpose and begins to govern our emotions, decisions, and interactions. The fallout of such unchecked desire is far-reaching, often leaving scars on our mental health, relationships, and self-perception. To understand the emotional toll it takes, one must delve into how it manifests and shapes the way we view ourselves, others, and the world around us.

One of the first effects of unchecked desire is the emergence of chronic dissatisfaction. When desire is allowed to dominate without limits, it creates a relentless cycle of pursuit and acquisition. Each new milestone, achievement, or possession may bring fleeting satisfaction, but that sense of fulfillment quickly fades, replaced by an even stronger craving for the next thing. This insatiable hunger leaves a person perpetually dissatisfied, unable to appreciate or enjoy what they already have. The focus shifts entirely to what is missing, what is just out of reach, and what could be obtained next. Life becomes a series of "if only" statements: if only I had that job, that car, that relationship, I would be happy. But the truth is, happiness remains elusive because the root of the dissatisfaction isn't external—it lies in the unchecked nature of the desire itself.

This chronic dissatisfaction often leads to feelings of inadequacy and self-doubt. When the object of desire becomes the benchmark for success or worth, failing to attain it—or even attaining it but finding it doesn't bring the expected fulfillment—can trigger a deep sense of failure. The individual begins to question their abilities, their choices, and even their value as a person. This is particularly true when the desire is tied to societal expectations or external validation. For example, someone consumed by the desire for career success might measure their self-worth entirely by promotions or accolades. If those markers are not achieved, or if they are achieved but fail to bring happiness, it can leave the person feeling hollow, as though they are not enough. Over time, this persistent self-doubt can erode confidence and create a damaging inner narrative that is difficult to escape.

Unchecked desire also has a way of distorting priorities, which can lead to significant emotional strain. When a single pursuit takes precedence over all else, it often comes at the expense of other aspects of life that provide balance and joy. Relationships, self-care, hobbies, and personal growth are frequently neglected in favor of the desire in question. This imbalance creates a sense of emptiness, as the individual becomes disconnected from the things that once brought them happiness and stability. The emotional fallout is compounded by guilt—guilt for neglecting loved ones, for abandoning passions, or for losing touch with one's own identity. This guilt, while often suppressed or rationalized in the moment, has a way of resurfacing later, adding to the emotional burden.

Another aspect of the emotional fallout is the strain on personal relationships. Unchecked desire can make a person seem distant, preoccupied, or even selfish to those around them. Friends and family members may feel sidelined, as though they are less important than the object of desire. This perception, whether accurate or not, can create tension and resentment, leading to conflicts that further isolate the individual. In some cases, unchecked desire can even lead to the exploitation of relationships, as the person becomes so fixated on their goal that they begin to use others as a means to an end. For example, someone consumed by the desire for success might manipulate colleagues or neglect their partner's emotional needs, justifying these actions as necessary sacrifices. These behaviors, however, often leave lasting damage, eroding trust and intimacy over time.

The emotional toll of unchecked desire is also evident in the way it fosters anxiety and stress. The relentless pursuit of a goal, especially one that feels unattainable or distant, creates an undercurrent of tension that permeates daily life. There is a constant pressure to do more, achieve more, and be more, which can leave a person feeling perpetually on edge. This anxiety is often accompanied by fear—fear of failure, fear of judgment, or fear of losing what has already been gained. These fears create a mental environment that is anything but conducive to happiness or well-being. Instead of feeling energized or motivated, the individual becomes trapped in a cycle of worry and overthinking, unable to find peace even in moments of rest.

One of the more insidious effects of unchecked desire is the way it distorts self-perception. When desire becomes the central focus of life, it often leads to a narrowing of identity. The person becomes defined not by who they are but by what they want or what they are striving for. This reductionist view of self can be incredibly damaging, as it ignores the complexity and richness of the individual. It creates a fragile sense of identity, one that is entirely dependent on external factors. When those factors shift—when the object of desire is lost, unattainable, or fails to bring satisfaction—the individual is left with a sense of emptiness, unsure of who they are without their pursuit. This loss of self can be deeply unsettling, triggering an existential crisis that is difficult to navigate.

Unchecked desire also has a way of breeding resentment. When the pursuit of desire doesn't yield the expected results, it's natural to look for someone or something to blame. This resentment can be directed outward, toward others who are perceived as obstacles or competitors, or inward, toward oneself for perceived inadequacies. In either case, the resentment only adds to the emotional burden, creating a toxic cycle of anger and frustration. This bitterness can seep into other areas of life, affecting relationships, work, and even one's overall outlook on life. It becomes increasingly difficult to find joy or gratitude when resentment is allowed to take root.

The emotional fallout of unchecked desire is further exacerbated by its tendency to isolate. As the individual becomes more consumed by their pursuit, they often withdraw from social connections and support systems. This isolation creates a feedback loop, where the lack of external perspective reinforces the intensity of the desire. Without the grounding influence of loved ones or the balance provided by diverse interests, the person becomes more entrenched in their pursuit, making it even harder to step back and reassess. The loneliness that results is both a symptom and a cause of the emotional fallout, as it leaves the individual feeling disconnected and unsupported.

Recovering from the emotional fallout of unchecked desire requires a deliberate and compassionate approach. It starts with self-awareness—recognizing the signs of imbalance and acknowledging the toll it has taken. This awareness creates the space for reflection, allowing the individual to reassess their priorities and reconnect with their values. It often involves setting boundaries, not just with others but with oneself, to ensure that desire remains a motivating force rather than a dominating one. Rebuilding relationships, practicing gratitude, and seeking support are also crucial steps in the healing process. By addressing the underlying issues and creating a more balanced approach to longing, it is possible to mitigate the emotional fallout and rediscover a sense of fulfillment and peace.

Chapter 4: Love and Lust Where They Collide

The Thin Line Between Lust and Love

The line between lust and love is as thin as it is complex, often blurred by the intensity of emotions and desires that accompany human connection. Lust can be dazzlingly immediate, a visceral and almost primal attraction that ignites the senses and consumes the mind. Love, on the other hand, unfolds more gradually, building its foundation on shared understanding, trust, and emotional depth. Yet, distinguishing between the two can be one of the greatest challenges of relationships, as the intoxicating nature of lust often masquerades as the beginnings of love. The difficulty lies not only in identifying the differences but also in understanding how these two forces can coexist, intermingle, and at times, conflict within the same relationship.

Lust is driven by physical attraction and the thrill of novelty. It is the spark that draws people together, a magnetic pull that feels both exhilarating and all-encompassing. This intensity can create a false sense of connection, making it easy to mistake lust for love. When you're caught up in the whirlwind of passion, it's tempting to believe that the depth of your feelings must signify something profound. Lust, however, is often more about the self than the other person. It feeds on fantasy, projecting idealized qualities onto the object of desire. What you feel may not be a genuine connection to who the other person truly is, but rather an infatuation with who you imagine them to be.

Love, in contrast, is rooted in reality. It grows not from the heat of passion but from the steady warmth of shared experiences and mutual care. While lust is largely about what you can get—pleasure, excitement, validation—love is about what you can give. It requires vulnerability, patience, and a willingness to invest in someone else's happiness and well-being. Love sees the flaws and imperfections in another person and chooses to accept them, whereas lust often fades when the initial allure begins to wear off. Where lust is fleeting and often conditional, love endures, thriving on trust and emotional intimacy.

The thin line between these two states becomes even more challenging to navigate when they overlap. Lust often acts as the gateway to love, providing the initial spark that draws people together. In healthy relationships, this physical attraction evolves into a deeper emotional connection, with lust and love complementing one another. However, problems arise when the balance tips too far in one direction. A relationship built solely on lust may lack the emotional depth necessary to sustain it, leading to disappointment or heartbreak once the initial excitement fades. Conversely, a relationship devoid of physical attraction may struggle to maintain passion and intimacy, leaving both partners feeling unfulfilled.

One of the key differences between lust and love lies in the way they influence your behavior and decision-making. Lust is impulsive and often disregards logic or long-term consequences. It thrives on immediacy, urging you to act on your desires without fully considering the implications. This can lead to rushed decisions, such as entering a relationship prematurely or ignoring red flags because the physical chemistry is so compelling. Love, on the other hand, encourages thoughtfulness and consideration. It takes into account the needs and feelings of both partners, fostering a sense of mutual respect and understanding. While lust may push you to focus on the present moment, love asks you to think about the future and what it takes to build a lasting connection.

Another distinguishing factor is the emotional impact of each. Lust, while exhilarating, can also be destabilizing. Its intensity can create feelings of obsession, insecurity, or even jealousy, particularly if the object of your desire does not reciprocate your feelings. Love, by contrast, is steadier and more grounding. It provides a sense of safety and belonging, offering emotional support and stability. While lust often leaves you wanting more, love fulfills the deeper human need for connection and companionship.

The interplay between lust and love can be further complicated by societal and cultural influences. Media and popular culture often romanticize the idea of love at first sight, blurring the line between physical attraction and emotional connection. These portrayals can create unrealistic expectations, leading people to equate the intensity of lust with the depth of love. In reality, love rarely happens instantly; it is a process that unfolds over time, requiring effort and commitment. Understanding this distinction is crucial

for navigating relationships and managing
expectations.

Recognizing whether your feelings stem from lust or
love requires introspection and honesty. Ask yourself
what draws you to the other person: Is it purely
physical, or do you feel a deeper emotional
connection? Do you find yourself fantasizing about
their appearance and the way they make you feel, or
do you genuinely care about their thoughts, feelings,
and well-being? Are you willing to make sacrifices for
their happiness, or is your focus primarily on what
they can offer you? These questions can help clarify
the nature of your feelings and guide your actions
accordingly.

It's also important to consider how the relationship
makes you feel about yourself. Lust often thrives on
external validation, making you feel desirable or
powerful in the presence of the other person. Love, on
the other hand, nurtures your sense of self-worth and
encourages personal growth. A loving relationship
should make you feel valued and supported, not just
admired or desired. If your connection leaves you
feeling insecure, anxious, or unfulfilled, it may be a
sign that lust is playing a larger role than love.

Navigating the thin line between lust and love also
involves communication and self-awareness. Be
honest with yourself and your partner about your
intentions and expectations. If you're unsure whether
your feelings are rooted in lust or love, take the time
to explore the relationship without rushing into
commitments. Building a foundation of trust and
understanding is essential for determining whether

your connection has the potential to grow into something more meaningful. At the same time, be mindful of the risks of staying in a relationship that is purely driven by lust, as it may prevent you from finding a connection that truly fulfills you.

It's worth noting that lust and love are not mutually exclusive, nor are they inherently in conflict. In fact, the most fulfilling relationships often involve a healthy blend of both. Passion and physical attraction can add excitement and energy to a relationship, while love provides the emotional depth and stability needed to sustain it. The key is to strike a balance, allowing both forces to coexist in a way that enhances rather than undermines the connection. This balance requires ongoing effort, communication, and a willingness to adapt as the relationship evolves.

Chemistry and Compatibility Do They Go Hand in Hand

Chemistry and compatibility are often used interchangeably when describing relationships, yet they are fundamentally different dimensions of human connection. Chemistry is the spark, the inexplicable force that draws people together. It's the electric jolt of attraction, the magnetic pull that makes your heart race and your mind fixate on someone. Compatibility, on the other hand, is the steady rhythm that sustains a partnership over time. It's the alignment of values, goals, and personalities that allows two individuals to coexist harmoniously. While chemistry can feel like destiny, compatibility is the product of conscious effort and understanding. The question that often arises is whether these two elements go hand in hand, or if they exist on separate planes, occasionally converging but just as often diverging.

Chemistry is immediate; it doesn't require explanation or analysis. It's that undeniable connection you feel when you lock eyes with someone across a crowded room, the way their presence seems to light up the space around you. This kind of attraction can be intoxicating, making it easy to believe that you've found something rare and profound. But chemistry, as powerful as it is, can also be deceptive. It operates on instinct and emotion, not logic or reason. It's entirely possible to feel a strong chemical pull toward someone who is fundamentally incompatible with you, someone whose values, priorities, or temperament clash with your own. This is where the distinction between chemistry and compatibility becomes crucial.

Compatibility, unlike chemistry, often takes time to reveal itself. It's not something you feel instantly; it's something you discover through shared experiences, open communication, and mutual respect. Compatibility is about whether two people can build a life together, not just share a fleeting moment of passion. It encompasses a wide range of factors, from how you handle conflict to how you envision your future. Do you share similar values when it comes to family, career, or finances? Are your communication styles complementary? Do you approach challenges as partners, or do you find yourselves at odds? These are the questions that determine compatibility, and they require time and effort to answer.

The interplay between chemistry and compatibility can be both fascinating and frustrating. In an ideal world, the two would always align: you'd feel an immediate spark with someone who also happens to share your values and life goals. But reality is often more complicated. There are times when you meet someone with whom you share incredible chemistry, only to discover that your lifestyles or priorities are fundamentally misaligned. Conversely, you might meet someone who is perfectly compatible with you on paper but with whom you feel no real spark. This disconnect can be disheartening, leading many to wonder whether they're asking for too much by expecting both chemistry and compatibility in a single relationship.

One of the reasons chemistry and compatibility don't always go hand in hand is that they are rooted in different parts of our psychology. Chemistry is largely driven by biology—it's influenced by hormones, pheromones, and subconscious cues that signal attraction. It's an evolutionary mechanism designed to bring people together, ensuring the continuation of the species. Compatibility, however, is rooted in emotional and intellectual connection. It's about whether two people can create a partnership that is fulfilling and sustainable over the long term. While chemistry is often immediate and visceral, compatibility requires introspection, communication, and compromise.

The challenge lies in balancing these two forces. Chemistry can be so compelling that it overshadows compatibility, leading people to overlook red flags or dismiss incompatibilities. It's easy to get swept up in the excitement of a new relationship, convincing yourself that the intensity of your feelings will somehow make up for any differences in values or goals. But this approach often leads to disappointment, as the initial spark of chemistry fades and the underlying incompatibilities come to the surface. On the other hand, focusing solely on compatibility without any chemistry can result in a relationship that feels more like a partnership than a romance. While there's nothing inherently wrong with this dynamic, it may leave one or both partners feeling unfulfilled, longing for the passion and excitement that chemistry brings.

Understanding the relationship between chemistry and compatibility requires a willingness to approach relationships with both your heart and your mind. It's important to honor the feelings of attraction and excitement that chemistry brings, but it's equally important to take a step back and evaluate whether the relationship has the foundation it needs to thrive. This means asking yourself tough questions about what you're looking for in a partner and being honest about whether the person you're drawn to aligns with those expectations. It also means being open to the possibility that chemistry can develop over time. While initial attraction is important, some of the most enduring relationships are those where chemistry grew out of a foundation of compatibility and mutual respect.

One way to navigate this balance is to pay attention to how the relationship evolves over time. Chemistry often burns bright in the early stages of a relationship, but it's compatibility that determines whether that initial spark can transform into something lasting. Do you find that your connection deepens as you get to know each other, or does the excitement fade as the novelty wears off? Are you able to navigate challenges together, or do your differences create conflict and tension? These are the kinds of questions that can help you discern whether chemistry and compatibility are working in tandem or pulling you in opposite directions.

It's also worth considering the role of timing in the interplay between chemistry and compatibility. Sometimes, you might meet someone with whom you share incredible chemistry, but the timing isn't right for a relationship. Perhaps one of you is in a different stage of life, or external circumstances make it difficult to build a partnership. In these cases, it's important to recognize that timing can be just as important as chemistry and compatibility. A relationship requires all three elements to align in order to thrive.

Ultimately, the goal is not to choose between chemistry and compatibility but to find a balance that works for you. This balance will look different for everyone, as each person values these elements differently. Some may prioritize the excitement and passion of chemistry, while others may place greater emphasis on the stability and alignment of compatibility. The key is to be honest with yourself about what you need and to approach relationships with an open mind and an open heart.

It's also important to remember that relationships are not static. Chemistry and compatibility can evolve over time, influenced by the effort and intention that both partners bring to the relationship. A strong foundation of compatibility can create the space for chemistry to flourish, just as the excitement of chemistry can inspire a deeper commitment to building compatibility. By nurturing both elements, you can create a relationship that is not only passionate but also enduring.

Physical Needs vs Emotional Fulfillment

The delicate balance between physical needs and emotional fulfillment is a cornerstone of human relationships, yet it is one of the most misunderstood and often neglected aspects of connection. Physical needs—the cravings that stem from biology and instinct—are primal and immediate. They manifest as the desire for touch, intimacy, and physical closeness, fulfilling not just the drive for reproduction but also the urge to feel wanted, attractive, and alive. Emotional fulfillment, however, exists on a different plane. It is the nourishment of the heart and mind, the deep sense of security, love, and understanding that comes from being truly seen and valued by another person. While these two elements are distinct, they are intricately linked, often feeding into each other in ways that can either strengthen or destabilize a relationship.

At its core, physical need is a basic human instinct. It is a natural part of our biology, a system hardwired to ensure the survival of the species. But beyond reproduction, the physical aspect of relationships plays a vital role in bonding and connection. Touch, for example, releases oxytocin, often referred to as the "love hormone," which fosters feelings of closeness and trust. Whether it's a fleeting kiss, a lingering embrace, or the more intimate moments shared between partners, physical contact has the power to bridge emotional gaps, reaffirm affection, and create a sense of belonging. It's no wonder then that when physical needs go unmet, individuals often feel a sense of disconnection or frustration, even if emotional fulfillment seems intact.

However, physical intimacy alone cannot sustain a relationship. Without emotional depth, the relationship risks becoming transactional, reduced to a mere exchange of physical gratification without the richness of shared understanding or mutual respect. Emotional fulfillment is the glue that holds relationships together, providing a foundation upon which physical intimacy can flourish. It's the feeling of being known, accepted, and cherished for who you are, beyond just the physical. It is the cumulative result of open communication, shared experiences, and unwavering trust. Emotional fulfillment allows partners to feel safe in their vulnerability, creating an environment where physical needs can be expressed and met freely, without fear of judgment or rejection.

The tension between physical needs and emotional fulfillment often arises when one is prioritized at the expense of the other. In some relationships, physical needs take center stage, overshadowing the emotional connection. This can occur for a variety of reasons, such as intense initial attraction, societal pressures that glorify physical intimacy, or even personal insecurities that drive individuals to seek validation through physical means. While this dynamic may work in the short term, it often leads to dissatisfaction over time. The lack of emotional depth can leave one or both partners feeling unfulfilled, as though something essential is missing.

Conversely, there are relationships where emotional fulfillment is emphasized to the point that physical needs are neglected. This imbalance can be just as detrimental, as it creates a sense of physical distance that can erode intimacy and connection. Humans are not purely emotional beings; the physical aspect of a relationship is equally important in maintaining closeness and passion. When physical needs are ignored, partners may feel unattractive or undesired, fostering insecurities that can spill over into other aspects of the relationship. Over time, this lack of physical intimacy can create a chasm that even the strongest emotional bond may struggle to bridge.

One of the most significant challenges in balancing physical needs and emotional fulfillment is the way these elements are influenced by individual differences. People prioritize and experience these needs differently based on factors such as personality, upbringing, and past experiences. For example, someone who grew up in an environment where affection was rarely expressed may place a higher value on physical touch as a way of feeling loved, while another person might prioritize emotional support and verbal affirmation. Understanding and respecting these differences is crucial for fostering harmony in a relationship. It requires open and honest communication about expectations, boundaries, and desires, as well as a willingness to adapt and compromise.

Cultural and societal influences also play a role in shaping the way physical needs and emotional fulfillment are perceived and pursued. In many cultures, physical intimacy is often portrayed as the ultimate expression of love, leading people to equate sexual satisfaction with relationship success. This narrative can create unrealistic expectations and put undue pressure on individuals to prioritize physical needs, sometimes at the expense of emotional depth. On the other hand, some cultural norms stigmatize open discussions about physical intimacy, placing a greater emphasis on emotional connection while ignoring the importance of physical closeness. Both extremes fail to capture the nuanced interplay between these two dimensions of a relationship, perpetuating misunderstandings and unmet needs.

The interplay between physical needs and emotional fulfillment becomes even more complex within the context of long-term relationships. Over time, the initial thrill of physical attraction often gives way to the steadier rhythms of daily life. This transition is natural and inevitable, but it can lead to challenges if not addressed with care. As familiarity grows, the intensity of physical desire may wane, making it essential for couples to actively nurture their connection. This doesn't mean trying to recapture the exact excitement of the early days but rather finding new ways to maintain intimacy and keep the relationship dynamic. Emotional fulfillment becomes even more critical during this stage, as it provides the stability and trust needed to navigate the ebbs and flows of physical intimacy.

It's also important to recognize that physical needs and emotional fulfillment are not static; they evolve over time and in response to life's circumstances. Stress, health issues, and major life changes can all impact a person's ability to meet or express these needs. For example, a demanding work schedule might leave one partner feeling emotionally distant, while a medical condition could affect physical intimacy. In such situations, it's vital for couples to approach each other with empathy and patience, understanding that these challenges are temporary and can be overcome with mutual effort and support.

Achieving a balance between physical needs and emotional fulfillment is not a one-size-fits-all endeavor. It requires ongoing effort, communication, and a willingness to adapt to the changing dynamics of the relationship. One practical approach is to view these needs as interconnected rather than separate. Physical intimacy can be a gateway to emotional closeness, just as emotional fulfillment can enhance the quality of physical connection. By nurturing both aspects simultaneously, couples can create a relationship that is both passionate and deeply meaningful.

Another key to balancing these needs is cultivating self-awareness and emotional intelligence. Understanding your own needs and being able to articulate them clearly is the first step toward fostering a healthy relationship. It's equally important to listen to and validate your partner's needs, even if they differ from your own. This mutual understanding creates a foundation of trust and respect, allowing both partners to feel valued and supported.

The Role of Time When Lust Evolves into Love

Time is an often underestimated yet paramount force in the evolution of relationships, particularly when lust begins its transformation into love. Lust, that immediate and all-encompassing physical desire, often sweeps people off their feet with its intoxicating intensity. It's raw, visceral, and thrilling, fueled by the novelty of attraction and the rush of chemistry. However, it is time that determines whether those initial sparks of lust can evolve into the steady, enduring flame of love. Time is more than just the ticking of a clock—it is the space in which depth, understanding, and emotional intimacy are cultivated. It is the quiet architect of love, gradually building a connection that can withstand the inevitable tests of life and relationships.

Lust, by its nature, is impatient. It thrives in the immediate, urging people to act on desire without hesitation. It's the glance that lingers a second too long, the magnetic pull that makes you want to close the distance between yourself and another person. In these moments, time seems irrelevant, even suspended, as the intensity of attraction takes over. But lust, no matter how powerful, is fleeting. It is a spark, not a steady flame, and it often fades as quickly as it ignites. Without the foundation that time provides, lust alone is rarely enough to sustain a relationship.

The role of time becomes evident in the shift from the superficial to the substantial. In the early stages of a relationship, lust often dominates, drawing attention to physical attraction and the excitement of newness. But as time passes, the focus begins to shift. The once-overwhelming allure of someone's appearance or charm is gradually replaced by curiosity about who they are beneath the surface. What are their values? What drives them? How do they respond to joy, anger, or sadness? Time allows these questions to be explored, revealing the layers of a person that cannot be discerned in the heat of passion. It is through this process that love begins to take root, growing alongside—or sometimes in spite of—the initial spark of lust.

One of the most significant ways that time facilitates the evolution of lust into love is by fostering vulnerability. Lust often thrives on a sense of performance, an unspoken pressure to present oneself in the best possible light. It's about impressing, seducing, and captivating the other person. Love, however, requires a different kind of courage—the courage to be seen as you truly are. Over time, the masks come off, and partners begin to share their fears, insecurities, and imperfections. This vulnerability creates a deeper connection, one that is based not on physical attraction alone but on mutual trust and understanding. It is in these moments of honesty and openness that love finds its footing, transforming the relationship from something fleeting into something enduring.

Time also reveals the compatibility—or lack thereof—that underpins a relationship. Lust can be blind to differences in values, priorities, or goals, as its focus is largely physical and immediate. But as the relationship progresses, these differences become harder to ignore. Time exposes whether two people can navigate conflicts, support each other's dreams, and build a shared vision for the future. It is through this process that partners discover whether their connection is built on a solid foundation or merely propped up by the allure of physical attraction. In this way, time acts as both a test and a teacher, guiding relationships toward either growth or dissolution.

The transition from lust to love is not always linear, nor is it guaranteed. There are relationships in which lust burns brightly for a time but fails to evolve into something deeper. This can happen for a variety of reasons: a lack of emotional compatibility, an unwillingness to invest in the relationship, or simply the realization that the connection was never meant to be more than a fleeting encounter. On the other hand, there are relationships where lust and love coexist, each enriching the other in a dynamic and balanced partnership. In these cases, time serves as the bridge between the two, allowing the intensity of lust to mellow into the warmth of love without extinguishing the initial spark.

Patience is essential in this process. The evolution of lust into love cannot be rushed or forced; it must unfold naturally, at its own pace. This requires a willingness to embrace the uncertainties and imperfections of the journey. There will be moments of doubt, where the intensity of lust may wane and the depth of love has not yet fully emerged. These moments can be unsettling, leading some to question whether the relationship is worth pursuing. But it is often in these in-between spaces that the most profound growth occurs. By giving the relationship the time it needs to evolve, partners create the opportunity for love to take hold in a way that is authentic and lasting.

Time also plays a crucial role in building shared experiences, which are the lifeblood of love. While lust is often fueled by novelty, love thrives on familiarity—the kind that comes from navigating life's highs and lows together. Whether it's celebrating milestones, weathering challenges, or simply spending quiet evenings in each other's company, these experiences create a tapestry of memories that strengthen the bond between partners. Over time, these shared moments become the foundation of the relationship, providing a sense of stability and continuity that lust alone cannot offer.

It's important to recognize that the role of time is not purely passive; it requires active participation from both partners. Time alone does not guarantee the evolution of lust into love. It is what you do with that time—how you communicate, connect, and invest in each other—that determines the outcome. This means being intentional about nurturing the relationship, whether through small acts of kindness, open and honest conversations, or simply making time for each other amidst the demands of daily life. By prioritizing the relationship and committing to its growth, partners can harness the power of time to deepen their connection and transform their initial attraction into something enduring.

The role of time is also evident in the way it shapes our understanding of love itself. In the throes of lust, love can feel like an abstract ideal, something that exists on the horizon but has not yet been fully realized. As time passes, however, love becomes more tangible. It reveals itself not in grand gestures or sweeping declarations but in the quiet, everyday moments that define a relationship. It's the way your partner remembers your favorite coffee order, the patience they show when you've had a tough day, or the way they make you feel safe simply by being present. These are the markers of love, and they can only be recognized and appreciated through the lens of time.

The Hearts Decision Choosing Love Over Desire

The heart's decision to choose love over desire is a profound crossroads, one that many find themselves navigating at some point in their lives. Desire, with its fiery and urgent pull, can be consuming. It's a force that speaks to the most primal parts of who we are, driven by instinct, passion, and a longing for immediate gratification. Love, however, is quieter, steadier, and far more enduring. It does not demand attention in the same way desire does, but its depth and stability have the power to transform lives. Choosing love over desire often means embracing complexity, sacrifice, and patience, as love requires far more than the fleeting satisfaction that desire offers. It is a choice that necessitates emotional maturity and a willingness to look beyond the surface to build something lasting.

Desire often masquerades as love in its initial stages. It's intoxicating, making you feel alive in ways you may have never experienced before. The rush of adrenaline, the quickened heartbeat, the way your thoughts are consumed by another person—all of this can easily be mistaken for love. But desire is inherently self-focused. It is about what you want, what you crave, and how someone else can fulfill those needs. While this intensity can feel powerful, it is also fleeting. The foundation of desire is built on novelty and attraction, both of which can wane over time. Love, by contrast, shifts the focus outward. It is not solely about what you receive but about what you give. Love is an act of commitment, compassion, and mutual respect, grounded in a shared understanding and a willingness to grow together.

The decision to choose love over desire is not always clear-cut, as the two often coexist in the early stages of a relationship. The spark of desire can ignite the journey toward love, creating the initial connection that draws two people together. But there comes a point when the nature of the relationship must evolve. This is the moment when the heart must decide whether to pursue the deeper, more enduring path of love or to remain caught in the fleeting allure of desire. This decision is rarely easy, as it requires introspection, honesty, and sometimes the courage to walk away from something that feels good in the moment but lacks the substance needed for a lasting connection.

One of the key differences between love and desire lies in their capacity to endure challenges. Desire thrives in moments of ease and excitement, but it often falters when faced with adversity. Love, however, is resilient. It is the force that holds two people together through life's inevitable trials, whether they be external pressures or internal conflicts. Choosing love over desire means prioritizing the long-term well-being of the relationship over short-term gratification. It means standing by your partner in moments of difficulty, even when it is inconvenient or uncomfortable. This kind of commitment requires a level of emotional maturity that desire alone cannot provide.

The process of choosing love also involves recognizing and addressing the limitations of desire. Desire is often fueled by idealization—the tendency to see someone through rose-colored glasses, focusing only on their most attractive qualities while ignoring their flaws. This idealization can create unrealistic expectations, setting the stage for disappointment when the reality of who someone is inevitably comes to light. Love, on the other hand, embraces the whole person, imperfections and all. It is about accepting someone for who they are, not just who you want them to be. This acceptance is what allows love to grow and deepen over time, creating a bond that is far more meaningful than the fleeting highs of desire.

Another critical aspect of choosing love over desire is the willingness to invest in emotional intimacy. Desire often operates on the surface, driven by physical attraction and the thrill of the new. Love, however, requires delving deeper. It demands vulnerability, honesty, and a genuine effort to understand and connect with your partner on an emotional level. This kind of intimacy cannot be rushed or forced; it develops gradually through shared experiences, open communication, and mutual trust. By prioritizing emotional connection over physical attraction, you lay the groundwork for a relationship that is both fulfilling and sustainable.

The heart's decision to choose love also involves a shift in perspective. Desire often focuses on the question, "What can this person do for me?" Love, by contrast, asks, "What can we build together?" This shift from individual gratification to collective growth is what distinguishes love from mere attraction. Love is not just about how someone makes you feel but about the life you create together. It is about shared dreams, mutual support, and a partnership that enriches both individuals in ways that extend far beyond physical desire.

There is also an element of sacrifice involved in choosing love over desire. Love requires compromise, patience, and a willingness to put the relationship above your own immediate wants. This does not mean losing yourself or neglecting your own needs but rather finding a balance that allows both partners to thrive. Desire, with its focus on instant gratification, often resists this kind of sacrifice. It is concerned with the present moment, not the future. But love looks ahead, considering not just what feels good now but what will sustain the relationship over time.

The journey toward choosing love over desire is not without its challenges. It requires confronting your own biases, fears, and insecurities. It means being honest with yourself about what you truly want and need in a relationship, as well as being willing to let go of connections that are built solely on desire. This process can be painful, as it often involves walking away from something that feels exciting or comforting in the moment. But the rewards of choosing love are immeasurable. Love offers a sense of security, belonging, and purpose that desire alone cannot provide. It is the foundation upon which lasting happiness is built.

Time plays a crucial role in the heart's decision to choose love over desire. In the early stages of a relationship, it can be difficult to distinguish between the two, as both are often intertwined. But as time passes, the nature of the connection becomes clearer. Desire may fade, but love endures, growing stronger as it is nurtured and tested. This is why patience is essential in making this decision. By allowing the relationship to unfold naturally, you give yourself the opportunity to see whether it has the substance needed to transition from desire to love.

The decision to choose love over desire is ultimately a deeply personal one, shaped by your own values, experiences, and aspirations. There is no universal formula for making this choice, as every relationship is unique. But by approaching the decision with honesty, self-awareness, and a willingness to prioritize depth over superficiality, you increase your chances of finding a connection that is both passionate and enduring. Love is not always the easier choice, but it is the one that offers the greatest potential for growth, fulfillment, and lasting happiness.

Choosing love over desire does not mean abandoning passion or excitement. On the contrary, love has the capacity to deepen and enrich these elements in ways that desire alone cannot. When love and desire coexist, they create a relationship that is both grounded and dynamic, offering the best of both worlds. The key is to ensure that desire serves as a complement to love, not a substitute for it. By making the conscious decision to prioritize love, you create a foundation that allows passion to flourish within the context of a meaningful and enduring connection.

Chapter 5: Desire in Modern Relationships

Technology and Temptation The Role of Digital Love

The intersection of technology and human relationships has created a landscape that is as thrilling as it is treacherous. With the advent of smartphones, social media, dating apps, and virtual communication, the way people connect has evolved at an unprecedented pace. Technology has amplified the possibilities for love and connection, but it has also introduced a labyrinth of temptations that can challenge even the strongest relationships. Digital love—the pursuit or maintenance of romantic connections using technology—has become both a blessing and a complication, reshaping the very fabric of intimacy. The allure of instant gratification, the anonymity of online platforms, and the sheer breadth of options available at one's fingertips have all contributed to a delicate balancing act between genuine connection and the temptations that come with living in a hyper-connected world.

Dating apps have transformed the way people find partners, making it easier than ever to meet someone new. Swiping left or right has become second nature for millions, a process as casual as scrolling through social media. The promise of finding a perfect match has never felt so attainable, yet this convenience is not without its complexities. The abundance of options can foster a paradox of choice, where the sheer number of potential partners makes it difficult to commit to one. When every swipe opens the door to someone new, the temptation to keep searching—even when you've found someone promising—can be overwhelming. This endless pursuit of "better" creates a culture of disposable connections, where people are often treated as replaceable rather than as individuals worthy of time and effort.

Social media platforms, too, have reshaped the dynamics of love and temptation. On one hand, they allow couples to stay connected in ways that were once impossible. A simple message, a shared photo, or a comment can serve as a quick reminder of affection, even across great distances. On the other hand, social media has introduced new dimensions of insecurity and comparison. The curated lives of others, displayed in perfectly filtered photos and captions, can create unrealistic expectations for what love and relationships should look like. Partners may find themselves comparing their own relationships to the highlight reels of others, leading to dissatisfaction and doubt.

The anonymity and accessibility of online communication have also given rise to a new form of temptation: the digital flirtation. Whether it's through an Instagram direct message, a late-night text, or a chat on a dating app, technology has made it easier than ever to engage in interactions that blur the lines of fidelity. What starts as a harmless exchange can quickly escalate into something more, fueled by the illusion of detachment that comes with communicating through a screen. The temptation lies in the perceived lack of consequences—after all, how harmful can a few messages be? But these interactions can erode trust and intimacy, creating rifts that are difficult to repair.

Digital love is not limited to the pursuit of new connections; it also plays a significant role in maintaining existing relationships. Long-distance couples, for example, rely heavily on technology to bridge the physical gap between them. Video calls, voice messages, and shared playlists become lifelines, keeping the connection alive despite the miles that separate them. However, even in these situations, technology can be a double-edged sword. While it enables communication, it can also amplify feelings of loneliness and longing. The inability to be physically present with a partner can lead to frustration, and the reliance on digital communication can sometimes feel impersonal or insufficient.

One of the most significant challenges posed by technology in the realm of love is the concept of digital boundaries. In an age where people are constantly connected, the lines between personal and shared spaces can become blurred. Partners may feel entitled to access each other's social media accounts, read messages, or track each other's online activities. While transparency is an essential component of trust, the invasion of digital privacy can lead to feelings of resentment and mistrust. Striking a balance between openness and autonomy is crucial in navigating the complexities of digital love.

The role of technology in temptation cannot be overstated. Online platforms have created an environment where the temptation to stray is not only more accessible but also more discreet. Emotional affairs, once limited to physical proximity, can now unfold entirely online, often without the knowledge of one's partner. These digital dalliances may not involve physical intimacy, but they can be just as damaging, if not more so. The emotional investment in someone outside the relationship can create a sense of betrayal that is difficult to overcome.

Technology has also introduced the concept of "micro-cheating," a term used to describe seemingly minor actions that, while not overtly unfaithful, can still undermine trust. Liking an ex's photo on social media, engaging in flirtatious banter online, or maintaining secretive communication with someone outside the relationship are all examples of behaviors that can fall under this category. While these actions may seem insignificant in isolation, their cumulative effect can create tension and insecurity within a relationship.

Despite these challenges, technology also offers opportunities for strengthening love and connection. Couples can use digital tools to enhance their intimacy and communication. Sending thoughtful messages throughout the day, sharing memes that remind you of your partner, or creating shared digital albums of your favorite memories are all ways to use technology to foster closeness. Virtual date nights, where couples watch a movie together over video call or play online games, have become increasingly popular, especially during times when physical proximity is not possible. These small gestures can make a significant difference in maintaining a sense of connection and togetherness.

The rise of technology has also made it easier for people to access resources that can improve their relationships. Online therapy sessions, relationship coaching apps, and self-help platforms provide couples with tools to navigate challenges and strengthen their bond. These resources can be particularly beneficial for those who may not have access to traditional forms of support due to geographical or financial constraints.

To navigate the complexities of digital love and temptation, communication is key. Partners must engage in open and honest conversations about their expectations, boundaries, and concerns. Discussing topics such as social media usage, online interactions, and digital privacy can help establish a mutual understanding and prevent misunderstandings. It's important to approach these conversations with empathy and a willingness to compromise, recognizing that everyone's relationship with technology is unique.

Another crucial aspect of managing digital love is self-awareness. Understanding your own motivations and triggers can help you navigate the temptations that technology presents. For example, if you find yourself drawn to the validation of online attention, it may be worth exploring the underlying insecurities that drive this behavior. Similarly, if you feel threatened by your partner's online activities, examining the root of your jealousy can provide valuable insights into your own emotional landscape.

Open Relationships Redefining Desire in the 21st Century

The landscape of human relationships is undergoing a profound transformation, as our understanding of love, commitment, and intimacy evolves to accommodate the complexities of contemporary life. Open relationships, once relegated to the fringes of societal acceptance, are now emerging as a legitimate and increasingly discussed form of partnership. This shift reflects a broader cultural movement toward challenging traditional norms and embracing diversity in how individuals connect, love, and desire. While the concept of open relationships may seem radical to some, it is rooted in the timeless human need for both connection and freedom—two elements that, when balanced, can create deeply fulfilling partnerships.

At the heart of open relationships lies the redefinition of desire. For centuries, monogamy has been upheld as the gold standard of romantic commitment, often intertwined with cultural, religious, and societal expectations. Yet, for many individuals, monogamy can feel restrictive, particularly when it comes to acknowledging the natural ebb and flow of attraction. Open relationships challenge the notion that love and desire must be confined to a single partner. Instead, they offer a framework in which individuals can explore connections with others while maintaining a committed and honest partnership with their primary partner.

The motivations for pursuing an open relationship are as varied as the individuals who choose this path. For some, the decision stems from a desire to explore their sexuality and expand their understanding of intimacy. For others, it may be a practical solution to differences in libido, sexual orientation, or long-term compatibility. Open relationships can also provide a way to navigate the challenges of modern life, such as long-distance partnerships or demanding careers, by allowing partners to meet their emotional and physical needs in a way that feels authentic and sustainable.

Central to the success of an open relationship is communication. Unlike the often unspoken assumptions that underpin monogamous relationships, open partnerships require a heightened level of transparency and honesty. Partners must be willing to discuss their desires, boundaries, and expectations openly, even when these conversations are uncomfortable. This level of communication fosters trust and helps to prevent misunderstandings or feelings of betrayal. It also requires a commitment to ongoing dialogue, as the needs and boundaries of each partner may evolve over time.

Jealousy is perhaps one of the most significant challenges faced by individuals in open relationships. While it is often perceived as an inevitable and insurmountable obstacle, jealousy can be reframed as an opportunity for self-reflection and growth. By examining the root causes of jealousy—whether they stem from insecurity, fear of abandonment, or unmet needs—individuals can gain a deeper understanding of themselves and their relationships. In many cases, jealousy can be mitigated through clear agreements and consistent reassurance, as well as by cultivating a sense of compersion: the ability to feel joy and satisfaction for a partner's happiness and pleasure with someone else.

Establishing boundaries is another critical aspect of open relationships. These boundaries serve as a roadmap for navigating the complexities of non-monogamy, providing clarity and structure for both partners. Boundaries can take many forms, from agreements about the types of relationships or activities that are permitted, to guidelines about how much information is shared. Some couples may choose a "don't ask, don't tell" approach, while others may prefer full transparency. The key is to ensure that these boundaries are mutually agreed upon and reflect the needs and values of both partners.

Emotional intimacy is not diminished in open relationships; rather, it can be deepened through the practice of radical honesty and mutual respect. By allowing space for individual growth and exploration, open relationships can foster a sense of autonomy that strengthens the bond between partners. This autonomy does not mean a lack of commitment, but rather an acknowledgment that love and desire are expansive and multifaceted. In many cases, the freedom to explore connections with others can enhance the primary relationship, as partners return to each other with renewed appreciation and perspective.

Critics of open relationships often argue that they are unsustainable or inherently unstable. However, research and anecdotal evidence suggest otherwise. Numerous individuals and couples have reported long-term success in open partnerships, citing increased communication, personal growth, and sexual satisfaction as key benefits. It is worth noting that open relationships are not a one-size-fits-all solution and may not be suitable for everyone. The decision to pursue non-monogamy should be made with careful consideration and a clear understanding of one's own needs and values.

The rise of open relationships also reflects broader societal shifts in how we view relationships and commitment. In an era characterized by rapid globalization, technological advancement, and changing cultural norms, traditional models of partnership are being reexamined and reimagined. Open relationships are part of a larger movement toward embracing diversity and authenticity in all aspects of life, challenging the idea that there is a single "right" way to love.

Navigating an open relationship requires courage, self-awareness, and a willingness to confront deeply ingrained beliefs about love and fidelity. It also demands a high level of emotional intelligence, as partners must be able to navigate complex emotions and communicate effectively. For those who are willing to put in the effort, open relationships can offer a unique and fulfilling way to experience love and desire.

It is important to acknowledge that open relationships are not without their challenges. Miscommunication, unmet expectations, and emotional upheaval are potential pitfalls that require careful navigation. However, these challenges are not unique to non-monogamy; they are present in all relationships, regardless of structure. The difference lies in the willingness to approach these challenges with honesty, compassion, and a commitment to growth.

The future of open relationships is likely to be shaped by ongoing cultural and societal changes. As conversations about non-monogamy become more mainstream, there is an opportunity to challenge stigmas and misconceptions, fostering greater understanding and acceptance. This shift has the potential to create a more inclusive and compassionate world, in which individuals are free to define relationships on their own terms.

Social Medias Influence on Emotional Cravings

The digital age has reshaped nearly every aspect of human interaction, and perhaps no force has been more pervasive in this transformation than social media. Platforms like Instagram, Facebook, TikTok, and Twitter have not only altered the way we communicate but have also fundamentally impacted how we perceive ourselves, others, and our emotional needs. Social media's influence on emotional cravings is intricate and multifaceted, intertwining with our psychological wiring and societal constructs. At its core, these platforms tap directly into our innate desire for connection, validation, and belonging, amplifying these cravings and, in some cases, creating new ones.s are social creatures, wired to seek approval and connection from others. This primal need is rooted in our evolutionary history, where survival often depended on being part of a group. Social media has taken this instinct and magnified it to an extraordinary degree. Every like, comment, or share acts as a form of micro-validation, triggering a dopamine release in the brain. This chemical reaction provides a fleeting sense of reward, encouraging users to return to the platform for more. Over time, this creates a cycle of dependency, where individuals increasingly seek out these digital affirmations to satisfy their emotional cravings.

The curated nature of social media exacerbates this dynamic. Platforms are designed to showcase the highlights of life, creating an environment where users constantly compare themselves to others. Whether it's a picture-perfect vacation, a meticulously staged meal, or an announcement of professional success, these snapshots often fail to reflect the full reality of life. For the viewer, however, this curated content can generate feelings of inadequacy, envy, or longing. Emotional cravings for validation and self-worth may intensify as individuals attempt to measure up to the seemingly flawless lives of others.

Social media's algorithms further deepen these emotional impacts by prioritizing content that elicits strong reactions. Posts that provoke anger, outrage, or intense joy are more likely to appear in a user's feed, as these emotions drive higher engagement. This can create an emotional rollercoaster, where users are constantly exposed to content that stimulates intense feelings. Over time, this can desensitize individuals to more subtle or nuanced emotions, making them crave the instant gratification that comes from dramatic or sensational content.

The quest for validation on social media often manifests through a phenomenon known as "performative authenticity." Users may feel compelled to share personal struggles, vulnerabilities, or intimate moments in an effort to connect with others and gain approval. While this can foster a sense of community and understanding, it also creates a paradox. The act of sharing becomes less about genuine expression and more about crafting a narrative that will resonate with an audience. Emotional cravings for connection and recognition can lead individuals to prioritize external validation over internal reflection, potentially eroding their sense of self.

Social media has also redefined the way we experience relationships, both platonic and romantic. Platforms provide a constant stream of information about the lives of others, blurring the boundaries between public and private spheres. This can create feelings of intimacy with individuals we barely know while simultaneously fostering a sense of detachment in close relationships. Emotional cravings for connection may become fragmented, as users spread their attention across a vast network of acquaintances rather than focusing on deeper, more meaningful bonds.

The concept of "FOMO," or the fear of missing out, is another powerful driver of emotional cravings on social media. The constant exposure to others' experiences can create a sense of longing or dissatisfaction with one's own life. This fear can push individuals to engage with social media more frequently, seeking out content that will reassure them they are not being left behind. In doing so, they may inadvertently reinforce feelings of inadequacy, creating a cycle of emotional dependence on the platform.

For younger generations, who have grown up with social media as an integral part of their lives, the impact on emotional cravings is particularly pronounced. Adolescents and young adults are in a critical stage of identity formation, where external feedback plays a significant role in shaping self-perception. Social media provides a constant stream of feedback, often filtered through the lens of likes, comments, and followers. This can create a distorted sense of self-worth, where individuals equate their value with their online popularity. Emotional cravings for acceptance and belonging may become inextricably tied to their digital presence, making it difficult to separate their online and offline identities.

The rise of influencers and content creators has added another layer to this dynamic. These individuals often serve as aspirational figures, showcasing lifestyles, appearances, or achievements that many followers desire. While influencers can inspire and motivate, they can also exacerbate feelings of inadequacy or longing. Emotional cravings for success, beauty, or status may be heightened as users compare themselves to these idealized representations. The line between inspiration and unattainable aspiration can be thin, and navigating this distinction requires a level of self-awareness that many struggle to maintain.

Despite these challenges, social media is not inherently harmful. It has the potential to foster connection, spark creativity, and provide a platform for marginalized voices. The key lies in understanding and managing its influence on emotional cravings. Awareness is the first step in breaking the cycle of dependency. By recognizing how social media affects our emotions and behaviors, we can begin to set boundaries and reclaim control over our interactions with these platforms.

One practical approach is to cultivate mindfulness in social media use. This involves being intentional about the time spent on platforms and the content consumed. Instead of mindlessly scrolling, users can focus on engaging with content that aligns with their values and interests. Taking regular breaks from social media can also provide an opportunity to reconnect with the present moment and nurture offline relationships.

Another strategy is to challenge the narratives presented on social media. By recognizing that most content is curated and filtered, individuals can reduce the impact of comparison and focus on their own unique journey. Building self-worth from internal sources rather than external validation can help mitigate the emotional cravings that social media often amplifies.

Fostering deeper, more meaningful connections can also counteract the fragmentation of relationships caused by social media. Prioritizing face-to-face interactions, engaging in open and honest communication, and investing in a smaller circle of close relationships can provide the emotional fulfillment that digital connections often lack.

For parents and educators, guiding younger generations in navigating social media is crucial. Teaching digital literacy and encouraging critical thinking can help adolescents develop a healthier relationship with these platforms. Emphasizing the importance of self-reflection and intrinsic values can provide a foundation for resilience against the pressures of social media.

As the digital landscape continues to evolve, so too will its impact on emotional cravings. While social media has undoubtedly transformed the way we connect and communicate, it is up to individuals to determine how they engage with these platforms. By cultivating awareness, setting boundaries, and prioritizing authentic connections, it is possible to harness the benefits of social media while mitigating its potential pitfalls. In doing so, we can redefine the role of social media in our lives, ensuring that it serves as a tool for connection rather than a source of emotional dependence.

The Struggle for Authentic Connection in a Superficial World

Human beings are innately driven by the desire to connect, to feel seen and understood, to experience intimacy that transcends the ordinary. Yet, in a world increasingly dominated by surface-level interactions and curated personas, the pursuit of authentic connection has become an uphill battle. The struggle to find meaningful relationships—whether romantic, platonic, or even professional—has been compounded by societal pressures, digital influences, and a culture that often prioritizes appearance over substance. The result is a pervasive sense of loneliness and disconnection that coexists paradoxically with unprecedented access to others.

At the root of this issue is the emphasis on superficiality. Modern culture frequently rewards those who present themselves in ways deemed socially desirable, often at the expense of authenticity. Social media platforms, entertainment, and even workplace environments reinforce the idea that success and acceptance are tied to how well one can perform or conform. The pressure to project perfection—to amass likes, followers, or approval—has created an environment where vulnerability is often perceived as a weakness and where individuals feel compelled to hide their flaws.

This performative nature of modern interaction erodes the foundation of genuine connection. True intimacy requires honesty, openness, and the courage to reveal one's authentic self, including imperfections and insecurities. Yet, when people are conditioned to prioritize external validation over internal truth, they may hesitate to be vulnerable, fearing rejection or judgment. Relationships based on such facades lack the depth and trust necessary for meaningful connection, leaving individuals feeling isolated even in the presence of others.

The digital world, while offering immense opportunities for connection, has also contributed to the superficiality of interactions. Text messages, likes, and emojis cannot fully convey the nuances of human emotion or the depth of a face-to-face conversation. The convenience of digital communication often comes at the cost of genuine understanding. Misinterpretations are common, as tone and context are easily lost in text-based exchanges. Meanwhile, the curated nature of online profiles further distances individuals from their authentic selves, as they strive to present an idealized version that aligns with societal expectations.

The pursuit of authenticity is further hindered by the fast-paced nature of modern life. With schedules packed to the brim, many individuals struggle to find the time or energy to invest in deep relationships. Superficial interactions become a default, as meaningful connection requires effort, patience, and intentionality—qualities that are often sacrificed in the rush to meet deadlines, achieve goals, or simply keep up with daily responsibilities. This frantic pace leaves little room for the slow, deliberate process of building trust and understanding, making authentic relationships increasingly rare.

Cultural norms and societal expectations also play a significant role in shaping the struggle for genuine connection. In many contexts, vulnerability is stigmatized, particularly for men, who may be taught that expressing emotions is a sign of weakness. Women, too, face pressures to conform to unrealistic standards of perfection, both in appearance and behavior, which can discourage them from embracing their true selves. These gendered expectations perpetuate a cycle of superficiality, as individuals mask their authentic emotions and needs to fit prescribed roles.

The rise of consumerism has further complicated the quest for authenticity. In a society that equates worth with material possessions or achievements, individuals may feel compelled to project an image of success rather than seeking deeper, more meaningful forms of fulfillment. Relationships can become transactional, with individuals evaluating potential connections based on what they can gain rather than the intrinsic value of the relationship itself. This mindset undermines the mutual respect and empathy that are essential for authentic connection.

Despite these challenges, the yearning for genuine relationships persists. People crave the kind of connection that allows them to be fully themselves, to feel accepted and valued for who they truly are. The question, then, is how to navigate a world that often seems designed to thwart such connections. The answer lies in conscious effort and deliberate choices.

Cultivating authentic relationships begins with self-awareness. Before one can connect with others on a deep level, it is essential to understand and embrace one's own identity. This involves examining personal values, beliefs, and desires, as well as acknowledging and accepting vulnerabilities. Authenticity starts within, as individuals who are comfortable with themselves are better equipped to foster genuine connections with others. Self-acceptance creates a foundation of confidence and openness, allowing individuals to approach relationships without fear of judgment or rejection.

Vulnerability is a cornerstone of authentic connection. While it may feel risky to share one's true thoughts and feelings, doing so invites others to do the same, creating a space for mutual understanding and trust. Vulnerability fosters empathy, as it allows individuals to see and be seen in their full humanity. In a world that often prioritizes strength and perfection, embracing vulnerability can be a powerful act of courage that paves the way for deeper relationships.

Active listening is another crucial element in overcoming the barriers to authentic connection. In a culture that often prioritizes speaking over listening, taking the time to truly hear and understand others can set the stage for meaningful interaction. Active listening involves more than simply hearing words; it requires paying attention to nonverbal cues, asking thoughtful questions, and responding with empathy. By demonstrating genuine interest in others, individuals can create a sense of validation and belonging that strengthens the bond between them.

Setting boundaries is equally important in navigating the complexities of modern relationships. Authentic connection does not mean sacrificing one's own needs or values to please others. Instead, it involves finding a balance between openness and self-respect. Healthy boundaries create a framework for relationships that are both supportive and sustainable, ensuring that individuals can engage authentically without compromising their well-being.

Another vital step is to prioritize quality over quantity. In a world where social media often equates worth with the number of connections or followers, it can be tempting to focus on amassing a large network of acquaintances. However, deep, meaningful relationships are rarely found in numbers. By focusing on a smaller circle of trusted individuals, it becomes possible to invest the time and energy needed to build authentic connections.

Navigating the tension between superficiality and authenticity also requires challenging societal norms and expectations. This may involve questioning cultural narratives that equate worth with appearance, success, or material possessions. By rejecting these superficial metrics, individuals can shift their focus to the qualities that truly matter in relationships, such as empathy, trust, and shared values. This shift in perspective can open the door to more meaningful connections that are grounded in mutual respect and understanding.

The road to authentic connection is not without its challenges, but the rewards are profound. Genuine relationships have the power to transform lives, providing a sense of belonging, purpose, and fulfillment that cannot be found in surface-level interactions. By embracing vulnerability, practicing self-awareness, and prioritizing meaningful engagement, individuals can navigate the superficiality of modern life and rediscover the depth and richness of human connection.

The Future of Love and Desire in an Ever Changing Landscape

Love and desire have always been deeply entwined with the cultural, technological, and social contexts of their time. As the world continues to evolve at an unprecedented pace, so too does the way we experience and interpret these fundamental aspects of human existence. The future of love and desire is being shaped by a confluence of factors—shifting societal norms, technological advancements, and the growing emphasis on individual autonomy and personal fulfillment. These changes are dismantling long-held traditions and redefining how people connect, communicate, and express their innermost emotions. In this ever-changing landscape, the concept of love is becoming more fluid, and the ways in which we seek and fulfill desire are adapting to meet the complexities of modern life.

One of the most significant shifts is the loosening grip of traditional relationship models. For centuries, monogamous, heterosexual partnerships were regarded as the default framework for romantic love. Marriage, often tied to religious or economic imperatives, was seen as the ultimate marker of commitment and societal stability. However, the 21st century has ushered in an era of diversity and inclusivity, challenging these conventions and expanding the definition of love. People are increasingly questioning whether one-size-fits-all relationship structures truly serve their needs and desires. As a result, alternative relationship models— ranging from polyamory and open relationships to cohabitation without marriage—are gaining visibility and acceptance.

This evolution is driven, in part, by the growing recognition that love and desire are not static. They are dynamic forces that change over time, influenced by individual growth, life circumstances, and external pressures. The rigid frameworks of the past often left little room for this fluidity, leading to dissatisfaction, infidelity, or the dissolution of relationships. In contrast, the emerging emphasis on flexibility and communication allows individuals to navigate the complexities of love in a way that feels authentic and sustainable. This shift does not imply the abandonment of commitment or deep emotional connection but rather a reimagining of how these qualities are expressed and maintained.

Technology is playing a pivotal role in shaping the future of love and desire. The advent of dating apps and online platforms has revolutionized the way people meet and interact, offering unprecedented access to potential partners. These tools have made it easier than ever to connect with others who share similar interests, values, or goals, transcending geographical and social boundaries. However, they have also introduced new challenges. The abundance of choices can lead to decision fatigue, where individuals struggle to commit due to the perception that better options are always just a swipe away. This phenomenon, sometimes referred to as the "paradox of choice," underscores the importance of intentionality and self-awareness in navigating digital dating landscapes.

Beyond matchmaking, technology is also reshaping how desire is expressed and experienced. Advances in virtual reality, artificial companions, and other immersive technologies are creating new avenues for intimacy and exploration. These innovations have the potential to fulfill desires that may be difficult or impossible to achieve in traditional relationships, offering a safe space for experimentation and self-discovery. However, they also raise ethical and philosophical questions about the nature of connection and the boundaries between human and artificial interaction. As technology continues to evolve, society will need to grapple with these dilemmas, striking a balance between embracing innovation and preserving the essence of human intimacy.

The future of love and desire is also intertwined with broader societal changes, particularly the growing emphasis on individual autonomy and self-actualization. In the past, love was often framed as a self-sacrificial act, where individuals were expected to prioritize their partner's needs and desires above their own. While this approach can foster deep connection, it can also lead to resentment or the loss of personal identity. Today, there is a greater focus on maintaining a sense of self within relationships, recognizing that personal growth and fulfillment are essential components of a healthy partnership. This shift is reflected in the rise of concepts such as "self-love" and "relationship anarchy," which emphasize the importance of authenticity, consent, and mutual respect.

As societal norms continue to evolve, the intersection of love and identity is becoming increasingly complex. Issues of gender, sexuality, and cultural background are playing a more prominent role in shaping how individuals experience and express love. The growing visibility of LGBTQ+ relationships, for example, is challenging traditional narratives and paving the way for greater acceptance and understanding. Similarly, cross-cultural relationships are highlighting the richness and diversity of love, while also revealing the challenges of navigating differing traditions and expectations. These intersections underscore the need for empathy, open-mindedness, and a willingness to embrace the complexities of human connection.

The changing landscape of love and desire is not without its challenges. One of the most pressing concerns is the potential for disconnection in an increasingly digital world. While technology offers new opportunities for connection, it can also create barriers to intimacy. The prevalence of virtual communication, for instance, can sometimes lead to a lack of depth or authenticity in relationships. Similarly, the emphasis on instant gratification and convenience may undermine the patience and effort required to build lasting connections. To navigate these challenges, individuals will need to cultivate a sense of balance, integrating technology into their lives without allowing it to replace genuine human interaction.

www.ingramcontent.com/pod-product-compliance
Lightning Source LLC
Chambersburg PA
CBHW072011150726
47999CB00002B/600